NOTARY JOURNAL FOR ALL STATES

NOTARY NAME: _____

NOTARY SIGNATURE: _____

NOTARY ADDRESS: _____

_____

CITY _____ STATE _____ ZIP _____

BUSINESS PHONE: _____ -- _____ -- _____

HOME PHONE: _____ -- _____ -- _____

EMAIL: _____

RECORD OF NOTARIAL ACTS COVERED IN THIS JOURNAL FROM

START DATE: _____ END DATE: _____

COMMISSION NUMBER: _____ JURISDICTION: _____

DATE OF COMMISSION: _____ COMMISSION EXPIRATION DATE: _____

BOOK NO. _____

NOTES. _____

HOW TO MAKE AN ENTRY IN THIS NOTARY PUBLIC JOURNAL

NOTARY NAME: _____   COMMISSION NUMBER: _____

RECORD NO. 1	DOCUMENT TYPE/DATE	C	NOTARIZATION TYPE: ACKNOWLEDGEMENT / JURAT / OTH	D

DATE __(A)__

TIME ☐ AM ☐ PM

FEE __(B)__

THUMBPRINT

ID INFORMATION OR CREDIBLE WITNESS __(E)__

☐ PERSONAL KNOWLEDGE
☐ DL, PASSPORT OR OTHER ID CARD
☐ CREDIBLE WITNESS ID & SIGNATURE

PRINTED NAME & ADDRESS OF SIGNER __(F)__

ADDRESS OF NOTARY OR OTHER INFORMATION __(I)__

__(H)__

PHONE NO./EMAIL: __(G)__

SIGNATURE OF SIGNER __(J)__

X

A — Record the date and time that the signer appears before the Notary Public (including a.m. or p.m. designation).

B — Record the amount charged for the transaction including additional travel fees.

C — Record the "Title" or "Name" and date of document type. For Example: a Deed, Car Title, Power of Attorney, Grant, Joint Tenancy, Affidavit, etc.

D — Record the Notarization Act that is being performed. Most Notarization Acts will be Acknowledgement or Jurat, while others could be Copy Certification, Protest, and Oath of Office.

E — Record the ID of Signer or Credible Witness. Make sure to to record all relevant information and that it is in compliance with the laws in your state.

F — Record the name and address of Signer as typically seen on their ID. Verify that it's up to date.

G — Record the phone number of signer and email if needed.

H — Record the right thumbprint of individual seeking notary service if required by law of the particular state. See state laws for acceptable alternatives if necessary.

I — Record the address of Notary if required by state law or Other Information.

J — Record the signature of the individual having documents notarized. Verify that the signer's signature matches the one on their identification.

RECORD NO. 1	DOCUMENT TYPE/DATE	NOTARIZATION TYPE: ACKNOWLEDGEMENT / JURAT / OTHER
DATE	ID INFORMATION OR CREDIBLE WITNESS	PRINTED NAME & ADDRESS OF SIGNER
TIME ☐ AM ☐ PM		
FEE	☐ PERSONAL KNOWLEDGE ☐ DL, PASSPORT OR OTHER ID CARD ☐ CREDIBLE WITNESS ID & SIGNATURE	
THUMBPRINT	ADDRESS OF NOTARY OR OTHER INFORMATION	PHONE NO./EMAIL:
		SIGNATURE OF SIGNER
X

RECORD NO. 2	DOCUMENT TYPE/DATE	NOTARIZATION TYPE: ACKNOWLEDGEMENT / JURAT / OTHER
DATE	ID INFORMATION OR CREDIBLE WITNESS	PRINTED NAME & ADDRESS OF SIGNER
TIME ☐ AM ☐ PM		
FEE	☐ PERSONAL KNOWLEDGE ☐ DL, PASSPORT OR OTHER ID CARD ☐ CREDIBLE WITNESS ID & SIGNATURE	
THUMBPRINT	ADDRESS OF NOTARY OR OTHER INFORMATION	PHONE NO./EMAIL:
		SIGNATURE OF SIGNER
X

RECORD NO. 3	DOCUMENT TYPE/DATE	NOTARIZATION TYPE: ACKNOWLEDGEMENT / JURAT / OTHER
DATE	ID INFORMATION OR CREDIBLE WITNESS	PRINTED NAME & ADDRESS OF SIGNER
TIME ☐ AM ☐ PM		
FEE	☐ PERSONAL KNOWLEDGE ☐ DL, PASSPORT OR OTHER ID CARD ☐ CREDIBLE WITNESS ID & SIGNATURE	
THUMBPRINT	ADDRESS OF NOTARY OR OTHER INFORMATION	PHONE NO./EMAIL:
		SIGNATURE OF SIGNER
X

DOCUMENT TYPE/DATE	NOTARIZATION TYPE: ACKNOWLEDGEMENT / JURAT / OTHER	RECORD NO. 4

DATE	ID INFORMATION OR CREDIBLE WITNESS	PRINTED NAME & ADDRESS OF SIGNER
TIME ☐ AM ☐ PM		
FEE	☐ PERSONAL KNOWLEDGE	
	☐ DL, PASSPORT OR OTHER ID CARD	
THUMBPRINT	☐ CREDIBLE WITNESS ID & SIGNATURE	
	ADDRESS OF NOTARY OR OTHER INFORMATION	PHONE NO./EMAIL:
		SIGNATURE OF SIGNER
		X

DOCUMENT TYPE/DATE	NOTARIZATION TYPE: ACKNOWLEDGEMENT / JURAT / OTHER	RECORD NO. 5

DATE	ID INFORMATION OR CREDIBLE WITNESS	PRINTED NAME & ADDRESS OF SIGNER
TIME ☐ AM ☐ PM		
FEE	☐ PERSONAL KNOWLEDGE	
	☐ DL, PASSPORT OR OTHER ID CARD	
THUMBPRINT	☐ CREDIBLE WITNESS ID & SIGNATURE	
	ADDRESS OF NOTARY OR OTHER INFORMATION	PHONE NO./EMAIL:
		SIGNATURE OF SIGNER
		X

DOCUMENT TYPE/DATE	NOTARIZATION TYPE: ACKNOWLEDGEMENT / JURAT / OTHER	RECORD NO. 6

DATE	ID INFORMATION OR CREDIBLE WITNESS	PRINTED NAME & ADDRESS OF SIGNER
TIME ☐ AM ☐ PM		
FEE	☐ PERSONAL KNOWLEDGE	
	☐ DL, PASSPORT OR OTHER ID CARD	
THUMBPRINT	☐ CREDIBLE WITNESS ID & SIGNATURE	
	ADDRESS OF NOTARY OR OTHER INFORMATION	PHONE NO./EMAIL:
		SIGNATURE OF SIGNER
		X

RECORD NO. 7	DOCUMENT TYPE/DATE	NOTARIZATION TYPE: ACKNOWLEDGEMENT / JURAT / OTHER
DATE	ID INFORMATION OR CREDIBLE WITNESS	PRINTED NAME & ADDRESS OF SIGNER
TIME ☐ AM ☐ PM		
FEE	☐ PERSONAL KNOWLEDGE	
	☐ DL, PASSPORT OR OTHER ID CARD	
THUMBPRINT	☐ CREDIBLE WITNESS ID & SIGNATURE	
	ADDRESS OF NOTARY OR OTHER INFORMATION	PHONE NO./EMAIL:
		SIGNATURE OF SIGNER
		X

RECORD NO. 8	DOCUMENT TYPE/DATE	NOTARIZATION TYPE: ACKNOWLEDGEMENT / JURAT / OTHER
DATE	ID INFORMATION OR CREDIBLE WITNESS	PRINTED NAME & ADDRESS OF SIGNER
TIME ☐ AM ☐ PM		
FEE	☐ PERSONAL KNOWLEDGE	
	☐ DL, PASSPORT OR OTHER ID CARD	
THUMBPRINT	☐ CREDIBLE WITNESS ID & SIGNATURE	
	ADDRESS OF NOTARY OR OTHER INFORMATION	PHONE NO./EMAIL:
		SIGNATURE OF SIGNER
		X

RECORD NO. 9	DOCUMENT TYPE/DATE	NOTARIZATION TYPE: ACKNOWLEDGEMENT / JURAT / OTHER
DATE	ID INFORMATION OR CREDIBLE WITNESS	PRINTED NAME & ADDRESS OF SIGNER
TIME ☐ AM ☐ PM		
FEE	☐ PERSONAL KNOWLEDGE	
	☐ DL, PASSPORT OR OTHER ID CARD	
THUMBPRINT	☐ CREDIBLE WITNESS ID & SIGNATURE	
	ADDRESS OF NOTARY OR OTHER INFORMATION	PHONE NO./EMAIL:
		SIGNATURE OF SIGNER
		X

DOCUMENT TYPE/DATE	NOTARIZATION TYPE: ACKNOWLEDGEMENT / JURAT / OTHER	RECORD NO. 10

DATE	ID INFORMATION OR CREDIBLE WITNESS	PRINTED NAME & ADDRESS OF SIGNER
TIME ☐ AM ☐ PM		
FEE	☐ PERSONAL KNOWLEDGE	
	☐ DL, PASSPORT OR OTHER ID CARD	
THUMBPRINT	☐ CREDIBLE WITNESS ID & SIGNATURE	

ADDRESS OF NOTARY OR OTHER INFORMATION	PHONE NO./EMAIL:
	SIGNATURE OF SIGNER
	X

DOCUMENT TYPE/DATE	NOTARIZATION TYPE: ACKNOWLEDGEMENT / JURAT / OTHER	RECORD NO. 11

DATE	ID INFORMATION OR CREDIBLE WITNESS	PRINTED NAME & ADDRESS OF SIGNER
TIME ☐ AM ☐ PM		
FEE	☐ PERSONAL KNOWLEDGE	
	☐ DL, PASSPORT OR OTHER ID CARD	
THUMBPRINT	☐ CREDIBLE WITNESS ID & SIGNATURE	

ADDRESS OF NOTARY OR OTHER INFORMATION	PHONE NO./EMAIL:
	SIGNATURE OF SIGNER
	X

DOCUMENT TYPE/DATE	NOTARIZATION TYPE: ACKNOWLEDGEMENT / JURAT / OTHER	RECORD NO. 12

DATE	ID INFORMATION OR CREDIBLE WITNESS	PRINTED NAME & ADDRESS OF SIGNER
TIME ☐ AM ☐ PM		
FEE	☐ PERSONAL KNOWLEDGE	
	☐ DL, PASSPORT OR OTHER ID CARD	
THUMBPRINT	☐ CREDIBLE WITNESS ID & SIGNATURE	

ADDRESS OF NOTARY OR OTHER INFORMATION	PHONE NO./EMAIL:
	SIGNATURE OF SIGNER
	X

RECORD NO. 13	DOCUMENT TYPE/DATE	NOTARIZATION TYPE: ACKNOWLEDGEMENT / JURAT / OTHER
DATE	ID INFORMATION OR CREDIBLE WITNESS	PRINTED NAME & ADDRESS OF SIGNER
TIME ☐ AM ☐ PM		
FEE	☐ PERSONAL KNOWLEDGE ☐ DL, PASSPORT OR OTHER ID CARD ☐ CREDIBLE WITNESS ID & SIGNATURE	
THUMBPRINT		
	ADDRESS OF NOTARY OR OTHER INFORMATION	PHONE NO./EMAIL:
		SIGNATURE OF SIGNER
		X

RECORD NO. 14	DOCUMENT TYPE/DATE	NOTARIZATION TYPE: ACKNOWLEDGEMENT / JURAT / OTHER
DATE	ID INFORMATION OR CREDIBLE WITNESS	PRINTED NAME & ADDRESS OF SIGNER
TIME ☐ AM ☐ PM		
FEE	☐ PERSONAL KNOWLEDGE ☐ DL, PASSPORT OR OTHER ID CARD ☐ CREDIBLE WITNESS ID & SIGNATURE	
THUMBPRINT		
	ADDRESS OF NOTARY OR OTHER INFORMATION	PHONE NO./EMAIL:
		SIGNATURE OF SIGNER
		X

RECORD NO. 15	DOCUMENT TYPE/DATE	NOTARIZATION TYPE: ACKNOWLEDGEMENT / JURAT / OTHER
DATE	ID INFORMATION OR CREDIBLE WITNESS	PRINTED NAME & ADDRESS OF SIGNER
TIME ☐ AM ☐ PM		
FEE	☐ PERSONAL KNOWLEDGE ☐ DL, PASSPORT OR OTHER ID CARD ☐ CREDIBLE WITNESS ID & SIGNATURE	
THUMBPRINT		
	ADDRESS OF NOTARY OR OTHER INFORMATION	PHONE NO./EMAIL:
		SIGNATURE OF SIGNER
		X

DOCUMENT TYPE/DATE	NOTARIZATION TYPE: ACKNOWLEDGEMENT / JURAT / OTHER	RECORD NO. 16

DATE	ID INFORMATION OR CREDIBLE WITNESS	PRINTED NAME & ADDRESS OF SIGNER
TIME ☐ AM ☐ PM		
FEE	☐ PERSONAL KNOWLEDGE ☐ DL, PASSPORT OR OTHER ID CARD ☐ CREDIBLE WITNESS ID & SIGNATURE	
THUMBPRINT	ADDRESS OF NOTARY OR OTHER INFORMATION	PHONE NO./EMAIL:
		SIGNATURE OF SIGNER X

DOCUMENT TYPE/DATE	NOTARIZATION TYPE: ACKNOWLEDGEMENT / JURAT / OTHER	RECORD NO. 17

DATE	ID INFORMATION OR CREDIBLE WITNESS	PRINTED NAME & ADDRESS OF SIGNER
TIME ☐ AM ☐ PM		
FEE	☐ PERSONAL KNOWLEDGE ☐ DL, PASSPORT OR OTHER ID CARD ☐ CREDIBLE WITNESS ID & SIGNATURE	
THUMBPRINT	ADDRESS OF NOTARY OR OTHER INFORMATION	PHONE NO./EMAIL:
		SIGNATURE OF SIGNER X

DOCUMENT TYPE/DATE	NOTARIZATION TYPE: ACKNOWLEDGEMENT / JURAT / OTHER	RECORD NO. 18

DATE	ID INFORMATION OR CREDIBLE WITNESS	PRINTED NAME & ADDRESS OF SIGNER
TIME ☐ AM ☐ PM		
FEE	☐ PERSONAL KNOWLEDGE ☐ DL, PASSPORT OR OTHER ID CARD ☐ CREDIBLE WITNESS ID & SIGNATURE	
THUMBPRINT	ADDRESS OF NOTARY OR OTHER INFORMATION	PHONE NO./EMAIL:
		SIGNATURE OF SIGNER X

RECORD NO. 19	DOCUMENT TYPE/DATE	NOTARIZATION TYPE: ACKNOWLEDGEMENT / JURAT / OTHER
DATE	ID INFORMATION OR CREDIBLE WITNESS	PRINTED NAME & ADDRESS OF SIGNER
TIME ☐ AM ☐ PM		
FEE	☐ PERSONAL KNOWLEDGE	
	☐ DL, PASSPORT OR OTHER ID CARD	
THUMBPRINT	☐ CREDIBLE WITNESS ID & SIGNATURE	
	ADDRESS OF NOTARY OR OTHER INFORMATION	PHONE NO./EMAIL:
		SIGNATURE OF SIGNER
		X

RECORD NO. 20	DOCUMENT TYPE/DATE	NOTARIZATION TYPE: ACKNOWLEDGEMENT / JURAT / OTHER
DATE	ID INFORMATION OR CREDIBLE WITNESS	PRINTED NAME & ADDRESS OF SIGNER
TIME ☐ AM ☐ PM		
FEE	☐ PERSONAL KNOWLEDGE	
	☐ DL, PASSPORT OR OTHER ID CARD	
THUMBPRINT	☐ CREDIBLE WITNESS ID & SIGNATURE	
	ADDRESS OF NOTARY OR OTHER INFORMATION	PHONE NO./EMAIL:
		SIGNATURE OF SIGNER
		X

RECORD NO. 21	DOCUMENT TYPE/DATE	NOTARIZATION TYPE: ACKNOWLEDGEMENT / JURAT / OTHER
DATE	ID INFORMATION OR CREDIBLE WITNESS	PRINTED NAME & ADDRESS OF SIGNER
TIME ☐ AM ☐ PM		
FEE	☐ PERSONAL KNOWLEDGE	
	☐ DL, PASSPORT OR OTHER ID CARD	
THUMBPRINT	☐ CREDIBLE WITNESS ID & SIGNATURE	
	ADDRESS OF NOTARY OR OTHER INFORMATION	PHONE NO./EMAIL:
		SIGNATURE OF SIGNER
		X

DOCUMENT TYPE/DATE	NOTARIZATION TYPE: ACKNOWLEDGEMENT / JURAT / OTHER	RECORD NO. 22

DATE	ID INFORMATION OR CREDIBLE WITNESS	PRINTED NAME & ADDRESS OF SIGNER
TIME ☐ AM ☐ PM		
FEE	☐ PERSONAL KNOWLEDGE	
	☐ DL, PASSPORT OR OTHER ID CARD	
THUMBPRINT	☐ CREDIBLE WITNESS ID & SIGNATURE	
	ADDRESS OF NOTARY OR OTHER INFORMATION	PHONE NO./EMAIL:
		SIGNATURE OF SIGNER
		X

DOCUMENT TYPE/DATE	NOTARIZATION TYPE: ACKNOWLEDGEMENT / JURAT / OTHER	RECORD NO. 23

DATE	ID INFORMATION OR CREDIBLE WITNESS	PRINTED NAME & ADDRESS OF SIGNER
TIME ☐ AM ☐ PM		
FEE	☐ PERSONAL KNOWLEDGE	
	☐ DL, PASSPORT OR OTHER ID CARD	
THUMBPRINT	☐ CREDIBLE WITNESS ID & SIGNATURE	
	ADDRESS OF NOTARY OR OTHER INFORMATION	PHONE NO./EMAIL:
		SIGNATURE OF SIGNER
		X

DOCUMENT TYPE/DATE	NOTARIZATION TYPE: ACKNOWLEDGEMENT / JURAT / OTHER	RECORD NO. 24

DATE	ID INFORMATION OR CREDIBLE WITNESS	PRINTED NAME & ADDRESS OF SIGNER
TIME ☐ AM ☐ PM		
FEE	☐ PERSONAL KNOWLEDGE	
	☐ DL, PASSPORT OR OTHER ID CARD	
THUMBPRINT	☐ CREDIBLE WITNESS ID & SIGNATURE	
	ADDRESS OF NOTARY OR OTHER INFORMATION	PHONE NO./EMAIL:
		SIGNATURE OF SIGNER
		X

RECORD NO. 25	DOCUMENT TYPE/DATE	NOTARIZATION TYPE: ACKNOWLEDGEMENT / JURAT / OTHER
DATE	ID INFORMATION OR CREDIBLE WITNESS	PRINTED NAME & ADDRESS OF SIGNER
TIME ☐ AM ☐ PM		
FEE	☐ PERSONAL KNOWLEDGE	
THUMBPRINT	☐ DL, PASSPORT OR OTHER ID CARD ☐ CREDIBLE WITNESS ID & SIGNATURE	
	ADDRESS OF NOTARY OR OTHER INFORMATION	PHONE NO./EMAIL:
		SIGNATURE OF SIGNER
		X

RECORD NO. 26	DOCUMENT TYPE/DATE	NOTARIZATION TYPE: ACKNOWLEDGEMENT / JURAT / OTHER
DATE	ID INFORMATION OR CREDIBLE WITNESS	PRINTED NAME & ADDRESS OF SIGNER
TIME ☐ AM ☐ PM		
FEE	☐ PERSONAL KNOWLEDGE	
THUMBPRINT	☐ DL, PASSPORT OR OTHER ID CARD ☐ CREDIBLE WITNESS ID & SIGNATURE	
	ADDRESS OF NOTARY OR OTHER INFORMATION	PHONE NO./EMAIL:
		SIGNATURE OF SIGNER
		X

RECORD NO. 27	DOCUMENT TYPE/DATE	NOTARIZATION TYPE: ACKNOWLEDGEMENT / JURAT / OTHER
DATE	ID INFORMATION OR CREDIBLE WITNESS	PRINTED NAME & ADDRESS OF SIGNER
TIME ☐ AM ☐ PM		
FEE	☐ PERSONAL KNOWLEDGE	
THUMBPRINT	☐ DL, PASSPORT OR OTHER ID CARD ☐ CREDIBLE WITNESS ID & SIGNATURE	
	ADDRESS OF NOTARY OR OTHER INFORMATION	PHONE NO./EMAIL:
		SIGNATURE OF SIGNER
		X

DOCUMENT TYPE/DATE	NOTARIZATION TYPE: ACKNOWLEDGEMENT / JURAT / OTHER	RECORD NO. 28

DATE	ID INFORMATION OR CREDIBLE WITNESS	PRINTED NAME & ADDRESS OF SIGNER
TIME ☐ AM ☐ PM		
FEE	☐ PERSONAL KNOWLEDGE	
	☐ DL, PASSPORT OR OTHER ID CARD	
THUMBPRINT	☐ CREDIBLE WITNESS ID & SIGNATURE	
	ADDRESS OF NOTARY OR OTHER INFORMATION	PHONE NO./EMAIL:
		SIGNATURE OF SIGNER
		X

DOCUMENT TYPE/DATE	NOTARIZATION TYPE: ACKNOWLEDGEMENT / JURAT / OTHER	RECORD NO. 29

DATE	ID INFORMATION OR CREDIBLE WITNESS	PRINTED NAME & ADDRESS OF SIGNER
TIME ☐ AM ☐ PM		
FEE	☐ PERSONAL KNOWLEDGE	
	☐ DL, PASSPORT OR OTHER ID CARD	
THUMBPRINT	☐ CREDIBLE WITNESS ID & SIGNATURE	
	ADDRESS OF NOTARY OR OTHER INFORMATION	PHONE NO./EMAIL:
		SIGNATURE OF SIGNER
		X

DOCUMENT TYPE/DATE	NOTARIZATION TYPE: ACKNOWLEDGEMENT / JURAT / OTHER	RECORD NO. 30

DATE	ID INFORMATION OR CREDIBLE WITNESS	PRINTED NAME & ADDRESS OF SIGNER
TIME ☐ AM ☐ PM		
FEE	☐ PERSONAL KNOWLEDGE	
	☐ DL, PASSPORT OR OTHER ID CARD	
THUMBPRINT	☐ CREDIBLE WITNESS ID & SIGNATURE	
	ADDRESS OF NOTARY OR OTHER INFORMATION	PHONE NO./EMAIL:
		SIGNATURE OF SIGNER
		X

RECORD NO. 31	DOCUMENT TYPE/DATE	NOTARIZATION TYPE: ACKNOWLEDGEMENT / JURAT / OTHER
DATE	ID INFORMATION OR CREDIBLE WITNESS	PRINTED NAME & ADDRESS OF SIGNER
TIME ☐ AM ☐ PM		
FEE	☐ PERSONAL KNOWLEDGE	
	☐ DL, PASSPORT OR OTHER ID CARD	
THUMBPRINT	☐ CREDIBLE WITNESS ID & SIGNATURE	
	ADDRESS OF NOTARY OR OTHER INFORMATION	PHONE NO./EMAIL:
		SIGNATURE OF SIGNER
		X

RECORD NO. 32	DOCUMENT TYPE/DATE	NOTARIZATION TYPE: ACKNOWLEDGEMENT / JURAT / OTHER
DATE	ID INFORMATION OR CREDIBLE WITNESS	PRINTED NAME & ADDRESS OF SIGNER
TIME ☐ AM ☐ PM		
FEE	☐ PERSONAL KNOWLEDGE	
	☐ DL, PASSPORT OR OTHER ID CARD	
THUMBPRINT	☐ CREDIBLE WITNESS ID & SIGNATURE	
	ADDRESS OF NOTARY OR OTHER INFORMATION	PHONE NO./EMAIL:
		SIGNATURE OF SIGNER
		X

RECORD NO. 33	DOCUMENT TYPE/DATE	NOTARIZATION TYPE: ACKNOWLEDGEMENT / JURAT / OTHER
DATE	ID INFORMATION OR CREDIBLE WITNESS	PRINTED NAME & ADDRESS OF SIGNER
TIME ☐ AM ☐ PM		
FEE	☐ PERSONAL KNOWLEDGE	
	☐ DL, PASSPORT OR OTHER ID CARD	
THUMBPRINT	☐ CREDIBLE WITNESS ID & SIGNATURE	
	ADDRESS OF NOTARY OR OTHER INFORMATION	PHONE NO./EMAIL:
		SIGNATURE OF SIGNER
		X

DOCUMENT TYPE/DATE	NOTARIZATION TYPE: ACKNOWLEDGEMENT / JURAT / OTHER	RECORD NO. 34

DATE	ID INFORMATION OR CREDIBLE WITNESS	PRINTED NAME & ADDRESS OF SIGNER
TIME ☐ AM ☐ PM		
FEE	☐ PERSONAL KNOWLEDGE	
	☐ DL, PASSPORT OR OTHER ID CARD	
THUMBPRINT	☐ CREDIBLE WITNESS ID & SIGNATURE	
	ADDRESS OF NOTARY OR OTHER INFORMATION	PHONE NO./EMAIL:
		SIGNATURE OF SIGNER
		X

DOCUMENT TYPE/DATE	NOTARIZATION TYPE: ACKNOWLEDGEMENT / JURAT / OTHER	RECORD NO. 35

DATE	ID INFORMATION OR CREDIBLE WITNESS	PRINTED NAME & ADDRESS OF SIGNER
TIME ☐ AM ☐ PM		
FEE	☐ PERSONAL KNOWLEDGE	
	☐ DL, PASSPORT OR OTHER ID CARD	
THUMBPRINT	☐ CREDIBLE WITNESS ID & SIGNATURE	
	ADDRESS OF NOTARY OR OTHER INFORMATION	PHONE NO./EMAIL:
		SIGNATURE OF SIGNER
		X

DOCUMENT TYPE/DATE	NOTARIZATION TYPE: ACKNOWLEDGEMENT / JURAT / OTHER	RECORD NO. 36

DATE	ID INFORMATION OR CREDIBLE WITNESS	PRINTED NAME & ADDRESS OF SIGNER
TIME ☐ AM ☐ PM		
FEE	☐ PERSONAL KNOWLEDGE	
	☐ DL, PASSPORT OR OTHER ID CARD	
THUMBPRINT	☐ CREDIBLE WITNESS ID & SIGNATURE	
	ADDRESS OF NOTARY OR OTHER INFORMATION	PHONE NO./EMAIL:
		SIGNATURE OF SIGNER
		X

RECORD NO. 37	DOCUMENT TYPE/DATE	NOTARIZATION TYPE: ACKNOWLEDGEMENT / JURAT / OTHER
DATE	ID INFORMATION OR CREDIBLE WITNESS	PRINTED NAME & ADDRESS OF SIGNER
TIME ☐ AM ☐ PM		
FEE	☐ PERSONAL KNOWLEDGE ☐ DL, PASSPORT OR OTHER ID CARD ☐ CREDIBLE WITNESS ID & SIGNATURE	
THUMBPRINT	ADDRESS OF NOTARY OR OTHER INFORMATION	PHONE NO./EMAIL:
		SIGNATURE OF SIGNER
		X

RECORD NO. 38	DOCUMENT TYPE/DATE	NOTARIZATION TYPE: ACKNOWLEDGEMENT / JURAT / OTHER
DATE	ID INFORMATION OR CREDIBLE WITNESS	PRINTED NAME & ADDRESS OF SIGNER
TIME ☐ AM ☐ PM		
FEE	☐ PERSONAL KNOWLEDGE ☐ DL, PASSPORT OR OTHER ID CARD ☐ CREDIBLE WITNESS ID & SIGNATURE	
THUMBPRINT	ADDRESS OF NOTARY OR OTHER INFORMATION	PHONE NO./EMAIL:
		SIGNATURE OF SIGNER
		X

RECORD NO. 39	DOCUMENT TYPE/DATE	NOTARIZATION TYPE: ACKNOWLEDGEMENT / JURAT / OTHER
DATE	ID INFORMATION OR CREDIBLE WITNESS	PRINTED NAME & ADDRESS OF SIGNER
TIME ☐ AM ☐ PM		
FEE	☐ PERSONAL KNOWLEDGE ☐ DL, PASSPORT OR OTHER ID CARD ☐ CREDIBLE WITNESS ID & SIGNATURE	
THUMBPRINT	ADDRESS OF NOTARY OR OTHER INFORMATION	PHONE NO./EMAIL:
		SIGNATURE OF SIGNER
		X

DOCUMENT TYPE/DATE	NOTARIZATION TYPE: ACKNOWLEDGEMENT / JURAT / OTHER	RECORD NO. 40

DATE	ID INFORMATION OR CREDIBLE WITNESS	PRINTED NAME & ADDRESS OF SIGNER
TIME ☐ AM ☐ PM		
FEE	☐ PERSONAL KNOWLEDGE	
	☐ DL, PASSPORT OR OTHER ID CARD	
THUMBPRINT	☐ CREDIBLE WITNESS ID & SIGNATURE	
	ADDRESS OF NOTARY OR OTHER INFORMATION	PHONE NO./EMAIL:
		SIGNATURE OF SIGNER
		X

DOCUMENT TYPE/DATE	NOTARIZATION TYPE: ACKNOWLEDGEMENT / JURAT / OTHER	RECORD NO. 41

DATE	ID INFORMATION OR CREDIBLE WITNESS	PRINTED NAME & ADDRESS OF SIGNER
TIME ☐ AM ☐ PM		
FEE	☐ PERSONAL KNOWLEDGE	
	☐ DL, PASSPORT OR OTHER ID CARD	
THUMBPRINT	☐ CREDIBLE WITNESS ID & SIGNATURE	
	ADDRESS OF NOTARY OR OTHER INFORMATION	PHONE NO./EMAIL:
		SIGNATURE OF SIGNER
		X

DOCUMENT TYPE/DATE	NOTARIZATION TYPE: ACKNOWLEDGEMENT / JURAT / OTHER	RECORD NO. 42

DATE	ID INFORMATION OR CREDIBLE WITNESS	PRINTED NAME & ADDRESS OF SIGNER
TIME ☐ AM ☐ PM		
FEE	☐ PERSONAL KNOWLEDGE	
	☐ DL, PASSPORT OR OTHER ID CARD	
THUMBPRINT	☐ CREDIBLE WITNESS ID & SIGNATURE	
	ADDRESS OF NOTARY OR OTHER INFORMATION	PHONE NO./EMAIL:
		SIGNATURE OF SIGNER
		X

RECORD NO. 43	DOCUMENT TYPE/DATE	NOTARIZATION TYPE: ACKNOWLEDGEMENT / JURAT / OTHER
DATE	ID INFORMATION OR CREDIBLE WITNESS	PRINTED NAME & ADDRESS OF SIGNER
TIME ☐ AM ☐ PM		
FEE	☐ PERSONAL KNOWLEDGE	
THUMBPRINT	☐ DL, PASSPORT OR OTHER ID CARD ☐ CREDIBLE WITNESS ID & SIGNATURE	
	ADDRESS OF NOTARY OR OTHER INFORMATION	PHONE NO./EMAIL:
		SIGNATURE OF SIGNER
		X

RECORD NO. 44	DOCUMENT TYPE/DATE	NOTARIZATION TYPE: ACKNOWLEDGEMENT / JURAT / OTHER
DATE	ID INFORMATION OR CREDIBLE WITNESS	PRINTED NAME & ADDRESS OF SIGNER
TIME ☐ AM ☐ PM		
FEE	☐ PERSONAL KNOWLEDGE	
THUMBPRINT	☐ DL, PASSPORT OR OTHER ID CARD ☐ CREDIBLE WITNESS ID & SIGNATURE	
	ADDRESS OF NOTARY OR OTHER INFORMATION	PHONE NO./EMAIL:
		SIGNATURE OF SIGNER
		X

RECORD NO. 45	DOCUMENT TYPE/DATE	NOTARIZATION TYPE: ACKNOWLEDGEMENT / JURAT / OTHER
DATE	ID INFORMATION OR CREDIBLE WITNESS	PRINTED NAME & ADDRESS OF SIGNER
TIME ☐ AM ☐ PM		
FEE	☐ PERSONAL KNOWLEDGE	
THUMBPRINT	☐ DL, PASSPORT OR OTHER ID CARD ☐ CREDIBLE WITNESS ID & SIGNATURE	
	ADDRESS OF NOTARY OR OTHER INFORMATION	PHONE NO./EMAIL:
		SIGNATURE OF SIGNER
		X

DOCUMENT TYPE/DATE	NOTARIZATION TYPE: ACKNOWLEDGEMENT / JURAT / OTHER	RECORD NO. 46

DATE	ID INFORMATION OR CREDIBLE WITNESS	PRINTED NAME & ADDRESS OF SIGNER
TIME ☐ AM ☐ PM		
FEE	☐ PERSONAL KNOWLEDGE	
	☐ DL, PASSPORT OR OTHER ID CARD	
THUMBPRINT	☐ CREDIBLE WITNESS ID & SIGNATURE	
	ADDRESS OF NOTARY OR OTHER INFORMATION	PHONE NO./EMAIL:
		SIGNATURE OF SIGNER
		X

DOCUMENT TYPE/DATE	NOTARIZATION TYPE: ACKNOWLEDGEMENT / JURAT / OTHER	RECORD NO. 47

DATE	ID INFORMATION OR CREDIBLE WITNESS	PRINTED NAME & ADDRESS OF SIGNER
TIME ☐ AM ☐ PM		
FEE	☐ PERSONAL KNOWLEDGE	
	☐ DL, PASSPORT OR OTHER ID CARD	
THUMBPRINT	☐ CREDIBLE WITNESS ID & SIGNATURE	
	ADDRESS OF NOTARY OR OTHER INFORMATION	PHONE NO./EMAIL:
		SIGNATURE OF SIGNER
		X

DOCUMENT TYPE/DATE	NOTARIZATION TYPE: ACKNOWLEDGEMENT / JURAT / OTHER	RECORD NO. 48

DATE	ID INFORMATION OR CREDIBLE WITNESS	PRINTED NAME & ADDRESS OF SIGNER
TIME ☐ AM ☐ PM		
FEE	☐ PERSONAL KNOWLEDGE	
	☐ DL, PASSPORT OR OTHER ID CARD	
THUMBPRINT	☐ CREDIBLE WITNESS ID & SIGNATURE	
	ADDRESS OF NOTARY OR OTHER INFORMATION	PHONE NO./EMAIL:
		SIGNATURE OF SIGNER
		X

RECORD NO. 49	DOCUMENT TYPE/DATE	NOTARIZATION TYPE: ACKNOWLEDGEMENT / JURAT / OTHER
DATE	ID INFORMATION OR CREDIBLE WITNESS	PRINTED NAME & ADDRESS OF SIGNER
TIME ☐ AM ☐ PM		
FEE	☐ PERSONAL KNOWLEDGE	
	☐ DL, PASSPORT OR OTHER ID CARD	
THUMBPRINT	☐ CREDIBLE WITNESS ID & SIGNATURE	
	ADDRESS OF NOTARY OR OTHER INFORMATION	PHONE NO./EMAIL:
		SIGNATURE OF SIGNER
		X

RECORD NO. 50	DOCUMENT TYPE/DATE	NOTARIZATION TYPE: ACKNOWLEDGEMENT / JURAT / OTHER
DATE	ID INFORMATION OR CREDIBLE WITNESS	PRINTED NAME & ADDRESS OF SIGNER
TIME ☐ AM ☐ PM		
FEE	☐ PERSONAL KNOWLEDGE	
	☐ DL, PASSPORT OR OTHER ID CARD	
THUMBPRINT	☐ CREDIBLE WITNESS ID & SIGNATURE	
	ADDRESS OF NOTARY OR OTHER INFORMATION	PHONE NO./EMAIL:
		SIGNATURE OF SIGNER
		X

RECORD NO. 51	DOCUMENT TYPE/DATE	NOTARIZATION TYPE: ACKNOWLEDGEMENT / JURAT / OTHER
DATE	ID INFORMATION OR CREDIBLE WITNESS	PRINTED NAME & ADDRESS OF SIGNER
TIME ☐ AM ☐ PM		
FEE	☐ PERSONAL KNOWLEDGE	
	☐ DL, PASSPORT OR OTHER ID CARD	
THUMBPRINT	☐ CREDIBLE WITNESS ID & SIGNATURE	
	ADDRESS OF NOTARY OR OTHER INFORMATION	PHONE NO./EMAIL:
		SIGNATURE OF SIGNER
		X

DOCUMENT TYPE/DATE	NOTARIZATION TYPE: ACKNOWLEDGEMENT / JURAT / OTHER	RECORD NO. 52

DATE	ID INFORMATION OR CREDIBLE WITNESS	PRINTED NAME & ADDRESS OF SIGNER
TIME ☐ AM ☐ PM		
FEE	☐ PERSONAL KNOWLEDGE	
	☐ DL, PASSPORT OR OTHER ID CARD	
THUMBPRINT	☐ CREDIBLE WITNESS ID & SIGNATURE	

	ADDRESS OF NOTARY OR OTHER INFORMATION	PHONE NO./EMAIL:
		SIGNATURE OF SIGNER
		X

DOCUMENT TYPE/DATE	NOTARIZATION TYPE: ACKNOWLEDGEMENT / JURAT / OTHER	RECORD NO. 53

DATE	ID INFORMATION OR CREDIBLE WITNESS	PRINTED NAME & ADDRESS OF SIGNER
TIME ☐ AM ☐ PM		
FEE	☐ PERSONAL KNOWLEDGE	
	☐ DL, PASSPORT OR OTHER ID CARD	
THUMBPRINT	☐ CREDIBLE WITNESS ID & SIGNATURE	

	ADDRESS OF NOTARY OR OTHER INFORMATION	PHONE NO./EMAIL:
		SIGNATURE OF SIGNER
		X

DOCUMENT TYPE/DATE	NOTARIZATION TYPE: ACKNOWLEDGEMENT / JURAT / OTHER	RECORD NO. 54

DATE	ID INFORMATION OR CREDIBLE WITNESS	PRINTED NAME & ADDRESS OF SIGNER
TIME ☐ AM ☐ PM		
FEE	☐ PERSONAL KNOWLEDGE	
	☐ DL, PASSPORT OR OTHER ID CARD	
THUMBPRINT	☐ CREDIBLE WITNESS ID & SIGNATURE	

	ADDRESS OF NOTARY OR OTHER INFORMATION	PHONE NO./EMAIL:
		SIGNATURE OF SIGNER
		X

RECORD NO. 55	DOCUMENT TYPE/DATE	NOTARIZATION TYPE: ACKNOWLEDGEMENT / JURAT / OTHER
DATE	ID INFORMATION OR CREDIBLE WITNESS	PRINTED NAME & ADDRESS OF SIGNER
TIME ☐ AM ☐ PM		
FEE	☐ PERSONAL KNOWLEDGE	
THUMBPRINT	☐ DL, PASSPORT OR OTHER ID CARD ☐ CREDIBLE WITNESS ID & SIGNATURE	
	ADDRESS OF NOTARY OR OTHER INFORMATION	PHONE NO./EMAIL:
		SIGNATURE OF SIGNER X

RECORD NO. 56	DOCUMENT TYPE/DATE	NOTARIZATION TYPE: ACKNOWLEDGEMENT / JURAT / OTHER
DATE	ID INFORMATION OR CREDIBLE WITNESS	PRINTED NAME & ADDRESS OF SIGNER
TIME ☐ AM ☐ PM		
FEE	☐ PERSONAL KNOWLEDGE	
THUMBPRINT	☐ DL, PASSPORT OR OTHER ID CARD ☐ CREDIBLE WITNESS ID & SIGNATURE	
	ADDRESS OF NOTARY OR OTHER INFORMATION	PHONE NO./EMAIL:
		SIGNATURE OF SIGNER X

RECORD NO. 57	DOCUMENT TYPE/DATE	NOTARIZATION TYPE: ACKNOWLEDGEMENT / JURAT / OTHER
DATE	ID INFORMATION OR CREDIBLE WITNESS	PRINTED NAME & ADDRESS OF SIGNER
TIME ☐ AM ☐ PM		
FEE	☐ PERSONAL KNOWLEDGE	
THUMBPRINT	☐ DL, PASSPORT OR OTHER ID CARD ☐ CREDIBLE WITNESS ID & SIGNATURE	
	ADDRESS OF NOTARY OR OTHER INFORMATION	PHONE NO./EMAIL:
		SIGNATURE OF SIGNER X

DOCUMENT TYPE/DATE	NOTARIZATION TYPE: ACKNOWLEDGEMENT / JURAT / OTHER	RECORD NO. 58

DATE	ID INFORMATION OR CREDIBLE WITNESS	PRINTED NAME & ADDRESS OF SIGNER
TIME ☐ AM ☐ PM		
FEE	☐ PERSONAL KNOWLEDGE	
	☐ DL, PASSPORT OR OTHER ID CARD	
THUMBPRINT	☐ CREDIBLE WITNESS ID & SIGNATURE	
	ADDRESS OF NOTARY OR OTHER INFORMATION	PHONE NO./EMAIL:
		SIGNATURE OF SIGNER
		X

DOCUMENT TYPE/DATE	NOTARIZATION TYPE: ACKNOWLEDGEMENT / JURAT / OTHER	RECORD NO. 59

DATE	ID INFORMATION OR CREDIBLE WITNESS	PRINTED NAME & ADDRESS OF SIGNER
TIME ☐ AM ☐ PM		
FEE	☐ PERSONAL KNOWLEDGE	
	☐ DL, PASSPORT OR OTHER ID CARD	
THUMBPRINT	☐ CREDIBLE WITNESS ID & SIGNATURE	
	ADDRESS OF NOTARY OR OTHER INFORMATION	PHONE NO./EMAIL:
		SIGNATURE OF SIGNER
		X

DOCUMENT TYPE/DATE	NOTARIZATION TYPE: ACKNOWLEDGEMENT / JURAT / OTHER	RECORD NO. 60

DATE	ID INFORMATION OR CREDIBLE WITNESS	PRINTED NAME & ADDRESS OF SIGNER
TIME ☐ AM ☐ PM		
FEE	☐ PERSONAL KNOWLEDGE	
	☐ DL, PASSPORT OR OTHER ID CARD	
THUMBPRINT	☐ CREDIBLE WITNESS ID & SIGNATURE	
	ADDRESS OF NOTARY OR OTHER INFORMATION	PHONE NO./EMAIL:
		SIGNATURE OF SIGNER
		X

RECORD NO. 61	DOCUMENT TYPE/DATE	NOTARIZATION TYPE: ACKNOWLEDGEMENT / JURAT / OTHER
DATE	ID INFORMATION OR CREDIBLE WITNESS	PRINTED NAME & ADDRESS OF SIGNER
TIME ☐ AM ☐ PM		
FEE	☐ PERSONAL KNOWLEDGE	
	☐ DL, PASSPORT OR OTHER ID CARD	
THUMBPRINT	☐ CREDIBLE WITNESS ID & SIGNATURE	
	ADDRESS OF NOTARY OR OTHER INFORMATION	PHONE NO./EMAIL:
		SIGNATURE OF SIGNER
		X

RECORD NO. 62	DOCUMENT TYPE/DATE	NOTARIZATION TYPE: ACKNOWLEDGEMENT / JURAT / OTHER
DATE	ID INFORMATION OR CREDIBLE WITNESS	PRINTED NAME & ADDRESS OF SIGNER
TIME ☐ AM ☐ PM		
FEE	☐ PERSONAL KNOWLEDGE	
	☐ DL, PASSPORT OR OTHER ID CARD	
THUMBPRINT	☐ CREDIBLE WITNESS ID & SIGNATURE	
	ADDRESS OF NOTARY OR OTHER INFORMATION	PHONE NO./EMAIL:
		SIGNATURE OF SIGNER
		X

RECORD NO. 63	DOCUMENT TYPE/DATE	NOTARIZATION TYPE: ACKNOWLEDGEMENT / JURAT / OTHER
DATE	ID INFORMATION OR CREDIBLE WITNESS	PRINTED NAME & ADDRESS OF SIGNER
TIME ☐ AM ☐ PM		
FEE	☐ PERSONAL KNOWLEDGE	
	☐ DL, PASSPORT OR OTHER ID CARD	
THUMBPRINT	☐ CREDIBLE WITNESS ID & SIGNATURE	
	ADDRESS OF NOTARY OR OTHER INFORMATION	PHONE NO./EMAIL:
		SIGNATURE OF SIGNER
		X

DOCUMENT TYPE/DATE	NOTARIZATION TYPE: ACKNOWLEDGEMENT / JURAT / OTHER	RECORD NO. 64

DATE	ID INFORMATION OR CREDIBLE WITNESS	PRINTED NAME & ADDRESS OF SIGNER
TIME ☐ AM ☐ PM		
FEE	☐ PERSONAL KNOWLEDGE	
THUMBPRINT	☐ DL, PASSPORT OR OTHER ID CARD	
	☐ CREDIBLE WITNESS ID & SIGNATURE	
	ADDRESS OF NOTARY OR OTHER INFORMATION	PHONE NO./EMAIL:
		SIGNATURE OF SIGNER
		X

DOCUMENT TYPE/DATE	NOTARIZATION TYPE: ACKNOWLEDGEMENT / JURAT / OTHER	RECORD NO. 65

DATE	ID INFORMATION OR CREDIBLE WITNESS	PRINTED NAME & ADDRESS OF SIGNER
TIME ☐ AM ☐ PM		
FEE	☐ PERSONAL KNOWLEDGE	
THUMBPRINT	☐ DL, PASSPORT OR OTHER ID CARD	
	☐ CREDIBLE WITNESS ID & SIGNATURE	
	ADDRESS OF NOTARY OR OTHER INFORMATION	PHONE NO./EMAIL:
		SIGNATURE OF SIGNER
		X

DOCUMENT TYPE/DATE	NOTARIZATION TYPE: ACKNOWLEDGEMENT / JURAT / OTHER	RECORD NO. 66

DATE	ID INFORMATION OR CREDIBLE WITNESS	PRINTED NAME & ADDRESS OF SIGNER
TIME ☐ AM ☐ PM		
FEE	☐ PERSONAL KNOWLEDGE	
THUMBPRINT	☐ DL, PASSPORT OR OTHER ID CARD	
	☐ CREDIBLE WITNESS ID & SIGNATURE	
	ADDRESS OF NOTARY OR OTHER INFORMATION	PHONE NO./EMAIL:
		SIGNATURE OF SIGNER
		X

RECORD NO. 67	DOCUMENT TYPE/DATE	NOTARIZATION TYPE: ACKNOWLEDGEMENT / JURAT / OTHER
DATE	ID INFORMATION OR CREDIBLE WITNESS	PRINTED NAME & ADDRESS OF SIGNER
TIME ☐ AM ☐ PM		
FEE	☐ PERSONAL KNOWLEDGE	
THUMBPRINT	☐ DL, PASSPORT OR OTHER ID CARD ☐ CREDIBLE WITNESS ID & SIGNATURE	
	ADDRESS OF NOTARY OR OTHER INFORMATION	PHONE NO./EMAIL:
		SIGNATURE OF SIGNER
		X

RECORD NO. 68	DOCUMENT TYPE/DATE	NOTARIZATION TYPE: ACKNOWLEDGEMENT / JURAT / OTHER
DATE	ID INFORMATION OR CREDIBLE WITNESS	PRINTED NAME & ADDRESS OF SIGNER
TIME ☐ AM ☐ PM		
FEE	☐ PERSONAL KNOWLEDGE	
THUMBPRINT	☐ DL, PASSPORT OR OTHER ID CARD ☐ CREDIBLE WITNESS ID & SIGNATURE	
	ADDRESS OF NOTARY OR OTHER INFORMATION	PHONE NO./EMAIL:
		SIGNATURE OF SIGNER
		X

RECORD NO. 69	DOCUMENT TYPE/DATE	NOTARIZATION TYPE: ACKNOWLEDGEMENT / JURAT / OTHER
DATE	ID INFORMATION OR CREDIBLE WITNESS	PRINTED NAME & ADDRESS OF SIGNER
TIME ☐ AM ☐ PM		
FEE	☐ PERSONAL KNOWLEDGE	
THUMBPRINT	☐ DL, PASSPORT OR OTHER ID CARD ☐ CREDIBLE WITNESS ID & SIGNATURE	
	ADDRESS OF NOTARY OR OTHER INFORMATION	PHONE NO./EMAIL:
		SIGNATURE OF SIGNER
		X

DOCUMENT TYPE/DATE	NOTARIZATION TYPE: ACKNOWLEDGEMENT / JURAT / OTHER	RECORD NO. 70

DATE	ID INFORMATION OR CREDIBLE WITNESS	PRINTED NAME & ADDRESS OF SIGNER
TIME ☐ AM ☐ PM		
FEE	☐ PERSONAL KNOWLEDGE	
THUMBPRINT	☐ DL, PASSPORT OR OTHER ID CARD	
	☐ CREDIBLE WITNESS ID & SIGNATURE	
	ADDRESS OF NOTARY OR OTHER INFORMATION	PHONE NO./EMAIL:
		SIGNATURE OF SIGNER
		X

DOCUMENT TYPE/DATE	NOTARIZATION TYPE: ACKNOWLEDGEMENT / JURAT / OTHER	RECORD NO. 71

DATE	ID INFORMATION OR CREDIBLE WITNESS	PRINTED NAME & ADDRESS OF SIGNER
TIME ☐ AM ☐ PM		
FEE	☐ PERSONAL KNOWLEDGE	
THUMBPRINT	☐ DL, PASSPORT OR OTHER ID CARD	
	☐ CREDIBLE WITNESS ID & SIGNATURE	
	ADDRESS OF NOTARY OR OTHER INFORMATION	PHONE NO./EMAIL:
		SIGNATURE OF SIGNER
		X

DOCUMENT TYPE/DATE	NOTARIZATION TYPE: ACKNOWLEDGEMENT / JURAT / OTHER	RECORD NO. 72

DATE	ID INFORMATION OR CREDIBLE WITNESS	PRINTED NAME & ADDRESS OF SIGNER
TIME ☐ AM ☐ PM		
FEE	☐ PERSONAL KNOWLEDGE	
THUMBPRINT	☐ DL, PASSPORT OR OTHER ID CARD	
	☐ CREDIBLE WITNESS ID & SIGNATURE	
	ADDRESS OF NOTARY OR OTHER INFORMATION	PHONE NO./EMAIL:
		SIGNATURE OF SIGNER
		X

RECORD NO.	DOCUMENT TYPE/DATE	NOTARIZATION TYPE: ACKNOWLEDGEMENT / JURAT / OTHER
73		
DATE	ID INFORMATION OR CREDIBLE WITNESS	PRINTED NAME & ADDRESS OF SIGNER
TIME ☐ AM ☐ PM		
FEE	☐ PERSONAL KNOWLEDGE	
	☐ DL, PASSPORT OR OTHER ID CARD	
THUMBPRINT	☐ CREDIBLE WITNESS ID & SIGNATURE	
	ADDRESS OF NOTARY OR OTHER INFORMATION	PHONE NO./EMAIL:
		SIGNATURE OF SIGNER
		X

RECORD NO.	DOCUMENT TYPE/DATE	NOTARIZATION TYPE: ACKNOWLEDGEMENT / JURAT / OTHER
74		
DATE	ID INFORMATION OR CREDIBLE WITNESS	PRINTED NAME & ADDRESS OF SIGNER
TIME ☐ AM ☐ PM		
FEE	☐ PERSONAL KNOWLEDGE	
	☐ DL, PASSPORT OR OTHER ID CARD	
THUMBPRINT	☐ CREDIBLE WITNESS ID & SIGNATURE	
	ADDRESS OF NOTARY OR OTHER INFORMATION	PHONE NO./EMAIL:
		SIGNATURE OF SIGNER
		X

RECORD NO.	DOCUMENT TYPE/DATE	NOTARIZATION TYPE: ACKNOWLEDGEMENT / JURAT / OTHER
75		
DATE	ID INFORMATION OR CREDIBLE WITNESS	PRINTED NAME & ADDRESS OF SIGNER
TIME ☐ AM ☐ PM		
FEE	☐ PERSONAL KNOWLEDGE	
	☐ DL, PASSPORT OR OTHER ID CARD	
THUMBPRINT	☐ CREDIBLE WITNESS ID & SIGNATURE	
	ADDRESS OF NOTARY OR OTHER INFORMATION	PHONE NO./EMAIL:
		SIGNATURE OF SIGNER
		X

DOCUMENT TYPE/DATE	NOTARIZATION TYPE: ACKNOWLEDGEMENT / JURAT / OTHER	RECORD NO. 76

DATE	ID INFORMATION OR CREDIBLE WITNESS	PRINTED NAME & ADDRESS OF SIGNER
TIME ☐ AM ☐ PM		
FEE	☐ PERSONAL KNOWLEDGE	
	☐ DL, PASSPORT OR OTHER ID CARD	
THUMBPRINT	☐ CREDIBLE WITNESS ID & SIGNATURE	

ADDRESS OF NOTARY OR OTHER INFORMATION	PHONE NO./EMAIL:
	SIGNATURE OF SIGNER
	X

DOCUMENT TYPE/DATE	NOTARIZATION TYPE: ACKNOWLEDGEMENT / JURAT / OTHER	RECORD NO. 77

DATE	ID INFORMATION OR CREDIBLE WITNESS	PRINTED NAME & ADDRESS OF SIGNER
TIME ☐ AM ☐ PM		
FEE	☐ PERSONAL KNOWLEDGE	
	☐ DL, PASSPORT OR OTHER ID CARD	
THUMBPRINT	☐ CREDIBLE WITNESS ID & SIGNATURE	

ADDRESS OF NOTARY OR OTHER INFORMATION	PHONE NO./EMAIL:
	SIGNATURE OF SIGNER
	X

DOCUMENT TYPE/DATE	NOTARIZATION TYPE: ACKNOWLEDGEMENT / JURAT / OTHER	RECORD NO. 78

DATE	ID INFORMATION OR CREDIBLE WITNESS	PRINTED NAME & ADDRESS OF SIGNER
TIME ☐ AM ☐ PM		
FEE	☐ PERSONAL KNOWLEDGE	
	☐ DL, PASSPORT OR OTHER ID CARD	
THUMBPRINT	☐ CREDIBLE WITNESS ID & SIGNATURE	

ADDRESS OF NOTARY OR OTHER INFORMATION	PHONE NO./EMAIL:
	SIGNATURE OF SIGNER
	X

RECORD NO. 79	DOCUMENT TYPE/DATE	NOTARIZATION TYPE: ACKNOWLEDGEMENT / JURAT / OTHER
DATE	ID INFORMATION OR CREDIBLE WITNESS	PRINTED NAME & ADDRESS OF SIGNER
TIME ☐ AM ☐ PM		
FEE	☐ PERSONAL KNOWLEDGE	
THUMBPRINT	☐ DL, PASSPORT OR OTHER ID CARD ☐ CREDIBLE WITNESS ID & SIGNATURE	
	ADDRESS OF NOTARY OR OTHER INFORMATION	PHONE NO./EMAIL:
		SIGNATURE OF SIGNER X

RECORD NO. 80	DOCUMENT TYPE/DATE	NOTARIZATION TYPE: ACKNOWLEDGEMENT / JURAT / OTHER
DATE	ID INFORMATION OR CREDIBLE WITNESS	PRINTED NAME & ADDRESS OF SIGNER
TIME ☐ AM ☐ PM		
FEE	☐ PERSONAL KNOWLEDGE	
THUMBPRINT	☐ DL, PASSPORT OR OTHER ID CARD ☐ CREDIBLE WITNESS ID & SIGNATURE	
	ADDRESS OF NOTARY OR OTHER INFORMATION	PHONE NO./EMAIL:
		SIGNATURE OF SIGNER X

RECORD NO. 81	DOCUMENT TYPE/DATE	NOTARIZATION TYPE: ACKNOWLEDGEMENT / JURAT / OTHER
DATE	ID INFORMATION OR CREDIBLE WITNESS	PRINTED NAME & ADDRESS OF SIGNER
TIME ☐ AM ☐ PM		
FEE	☐ PERSONAL KNOWLEDGE	
THUMBPRINT	☐ DL, PASSPORT OR OTHER ID CARD ☐ CREDIBLE WITNESS ID & SIGNATURE	
	ADDRESS OF NOTARY OR OTHER INFORMATION	PHONE NO./EMAIL:
		SIGNATURE OF SIGNER X

DOCUMENT TYPE/DATE	NOTARIZATION TYPE: ACKNOWLEDGEMENT / JURAT / OTHER	RECORD NO. 82

DATE	ID INFORMATION OR CREDIBLE WITNESS	PRINTED NAME & ADDRESS OF SIGNER
TIME ☐ AM ☐ PM		
FEE	☐ PERSONAL KNOWLEDGE	
	☐ DL, PASSPORT OR OTHER ID CARD	
THUMBPRINT	☐ CREDIBLE WITNESS ID & SIGNATURE	
	ADDRESS OF NOTARY OR OTHER INFORMATION	PHONE NO./EMAIL:
		SIGNATURE OF SIGNER
		X

DOCUMENT TYPE/DATE	NOTARIZATION TYPE: ACKNOWLEDGEMENT / JURAT / OTHER	RECORD NO. 83

DATE	ID INFORMATION OR CREDIBLE WITNESS	PRINTED NAME & ADDRESS OF SIGNER
TIME ☐ AM ☐ PM		
FEE	☐ PERSONAL KNOWLEDGE	
	☐ DL, PASSPORT OR OTHER ID CARD	
THUMBPRINT	☐ CREDIBLE WITNESS ID & SIGNATURE	
	ADDRESS OF NOTARY OR OTHER INFORMATION	PHONE NO./EMAIL:
		SIGNATURE OF SIGNER
		X

DOCUMENT TYPE/DATE	NOTARIZATION TYPE: ACKNOWLEDGEMENT / JURAT / OTHER	RECORD NO. 84

DATE	ID INFORMATION OR CREDIBLE WITNESS	PRINTED NAME & ADDRESS OF SIGNER
TIME ☐ AM ☐ PM		
FEE	☐ PERSONAL KNOWLEDGE	
	☐ DL, PASSPORT OR OTHER ID CARD	
THUMBPRINT	☐ CREDIBLE WITNESS ID & SIGNATURE	
	ADDRESS OF NOTARY OR OTHER INFORMATION	PHONE NO./EMAIL:
		SIGNATURE OF SIGNER
		X

RECORD NO. 85	DOCUMENT TYPE/DATE	NOTARIZATION TYPE: ACKNOWLEDGEMENT / JURAT / OTHER
DATE	ID INFORMATION OR CREDIBLE WITNESS	PRINTED NAME & ADDRESS OF SIGNER
TIME ☐ AM ☐ PM		
FEE	☐ PERSONAL KNOWLEDGE	
	☐ DL, PASSPORT OR OTHER ID CARD	
THUMBPRINT	☐ CREDIBLE WITNESS ID & SIGNATURE	
	ADDRESS OF NOTARY OR OTHER INFORMATION	PHONE NO./EMAIL:
		SIGNATURE OF SIGNER
		X

RECORD NO. 86	DOCUMENT TYPE/DATE	NOTARIZATION TYPE: ACKNOWLEDGEMENT / JURAT / OTHER
DATE	ID INFORMATION OR CREDIBLE WITNESS	PRINTED NAME & ADDRESS OF SIGNER
TIME ☐ AM ☐ PM		
FEE	☐ PERSONAL KNOWLEDGE	
	☐ DL, PASSPORT OR OTHER ID CARD	
THUMBPRINT	☐ CREDIBLE WITNESS ID & SIGNATURE	
	ADDRESS OF NOTARY OR OTHER INFORMATION	PHONE NO./EMAIL:
		SIGNATURE OF SIGNER
		X

RECORD NO. 87	DOCUMENT TYPE/DATE	NOTARIZATION TYPE: ACKNOWLEDGEMENT / JURAT / OTHER
DATE	ID INFORMATION OR CREDIBLE WITNESS	PRINTED NAME & ADDRESS OF SIGNER
TIME ☐ AM ☐ PM		
FEE	☐ PERSONAL KNOWLEDGE	
	☐ DL, PASSPORT OR OTHER ID CARD	
THUMBPRINT	☐ CREDIBLE WITNESS ID & SIGNATURE	
	ADDRESS OF NOTARY OR OTHER INFORMATION	PHONE NO./EMAIL:
		SIGNATURE OF SIGNER
		X

DOCUMENT TYPE/DATE	NOTARIZATION TYPE: ACKNOWLEDGEMENT / JURAT / OTHER	RECORD NO. 88

DATE	ID INFORMATION OR CREDIBLE WITNESS	PRINTED NAME & ADDRESS OF SIGNER
TIME ☐ AM ☐ PM		
FEE	☐ PERSONAL KNOWLEDGE	
	☐ DL, PASSPORT OR OTHER ID CARD	
THUMBPRINT	☐ CREDIBLE WITNESS ID & SIGNATURE	
	ADDRESS OF NOTARY OR OTHER INFORMATION	PHONE NO./EMAIL:
		SIGNATURE OF SIGNER
		X

DOCUMENT TYPE/DATE	NOTARIZATION TYPE: ACKNOWLEDGEMENT / JURAT / OTHER	RECORD NO. 89

DATE	ID INFORMATION OR CREDIBLE WITNESS	PRINTED NAME & ADDRESS OF SIGNER
TIME ☐ AM ☐ PM		
FEE	☐ PERSONAL KNOWLEDGE	
	☐ DL, PASSPORT OR OTHER ID CARD	
THUMBPRINT	☐ CREDIBLE WITNESS ID & SIGNATURE	
	ADDRESS OF NOTARY OR OTHER INFORMATION	PHONE NO./EMAIL:
		SIGNATURE OF SIGNER
		X

DOCUMENT TYPE/DATE	NOTARIZATION TYPE: ACKNOWLEDGEMENT / JURAT / OTHER	RECORD NO. 90

DATE	ID INFORMATION OR CREDIBLE WITNESS	PRINTED NAME & ADDRESS OF SIGNER
TIME ☐ AM ☐ PM		
FEE	☐ PERSONAL KNOWLEDGE	
	☐ DL, PASSPORT OR OTHER ID CARD	
THUMBPRINT	☐ CREDIBLE WITNESS ID & SIGNATURE	
	ADDRESS OF NOTARY OR OTHER INFORMATION	PHONE NO./EMAIL:
		SIGNATURE OF SIGNER
		X

RECORD NO. 91	DOCUMENT TYPE/DATE	NOTARIZATION TYPE: ACKNOWLEDGEMENT / JURAT / OTHER
DATE	ID INFORMATION OR CREDIBLE WITNESS	PRINTED NAME & ADDRESS OF SIGNER
TIME ☐ AM ☐ PM		
FEE	☐ PERSONAL KNOWLEDGE	
	☐ DL, PASSPORT OR OTHER ID CARD	
THUMBPRINT	☐ CREDIBLE WITNESS ID & SIGNATURE	
	ADDRESS OF NOTARY OR OTHER INFORMATION	PHONE NO./EMAIL:
		SIGNATURE OF SIGNER
		X

RECORD NO. 92	DOCUMENT TYPE/DATE	NOTARIZATION TYPE: ACKNOWLEDGEMENT / JURAT / OTHER
DATE	ID INFORMATION OR CREDIBLE WITNESS	PRINTED NAME & ADDRESS OF SIGNER
TIME ☐ AM ☐ PM		
FEE	☐ PERSONAL KNOWLEDGE	
	☐ DL, PASSPORT OR OTHER ID CARD	
THUMBPRINT	☐ CREDIBLE WITNESS ID & SIGNATURE	
	ADDRESS OF NOTARY OR OTHER INFORMATION	PHONE NO./EMAIL:
		SIGNATURE OF SIGNER
		X

RECORD NO. 93	DOCUMENT TYPE/DATE	NOTARIZATION TYPE: ACKNOWLEDGEMENT / JURAT / OTHER
DATE	ID INFORMATION OR CREDIBLE WITNESS	PRINTED NAME & ADDRESS OF SIGNER
TIME ☐ AM ☐ PM		
FEE	☐ PERSONAL KNOWLEDGE	
	☐ DL, PASSPORT OR OTHER ID CARD	
THUMBPRINT	☐ CREDIBLE WITNESS ID & SIGNATURE	
	ADDRESS OF NOTARY OR OTHER INFORMATION	PHONE NO./EMAIL:
		SIGNATURE OF SIGNER
		X

DOCUMENT TYPE/DATE	NOTARIZATION TYPE: ACKNOWLEDGEMENT / JURAT / OTHER	RECORD NO. 94

DATE	ID INFORMATION OR CREDIBLE WITNESS	PRINTED NAME & ADDRESS OF SIGNER
TIME ☐ AM ☐ PM		
FEE	☐ PERSONAL KNOWLEDGE	
THUMBPRINT	☐ DL, PASSPORT OR OTHER ID CARD	
	☐ CREDIBLE WITNESS ID & SIGNATURE	
	ADDRESS OF NOTARY OR OTHER INFORMATION	PHONE NO./EMAIL:
		SIGNATURE OF SIGNER
		X

DOCUMENT TYPE/DATE	NOTARIZATION TYPE: ACKNOWLEDGEMENT / JURAT / OTHER	RECORD NO. 95

DATE	ID INFORMATION OR CREDIBLE WITNESS	PRINTED NAME & ADDRESS OF SIGNER
TIME ☐ AM ☐ PM		
FEE	☐ PERSONAL KNOWLEDGE	
THUMBPRINT	☐ DL, PASSPORT OR OTHER ID CARD	
	☐ CREDIBLE WITNESS ID & SIGNATURE	
	ADDRESS OF NOTARY OR OTHER INFORMATION	PHONE NO./EMAIL:
		SIGNATURE OF SIGNER
		X

DOCUMENT TYPE/DATE	NOTARIZATION TYPE: ACKNOWLEDGEMENT / JURAT / OTHER	RECORD NO. 96

DATE	ID INFORMATION OR CREDIBLE WITNESS	PRINTED NAME & ADDRESS OF SIGNER
TIME ☐ AM ☐ PM		
FEE	☐ PERSONAL KNOWLEDGE	
THUMBPRINT	☐ DL, PASSPORT OR OTHER ID CARD	
	☐ CREDIBLE WITNESS ID & SIGNATURE	
	ADDRESS OF NOTARY OR OTHER INFORMATION	PHONE NO./EMAIL:
		SIGNATURE OF SIGNER
		X

RECORD NO. 97	DOCUMENT TYPE/DATE	NOTARIZATION TYPE: ACKNOWLEDGEMENT / JURAT / OTHER
DATE	ID INFORMATION OR CREDIBLE WITNESS	PRINTED NAME & ADDRESS OF SIGNER
TIME ☐ AM ☐ PM		
FEE	☐ PERSONAL KNOWLEDGE	
	☐ DL, PASSPORT OR OTHER ID CARD	
THUMBPRINT	☐ CREDIBLE WITNESS ID & SIGNATURE	
	ADDRESS OF NOTARY OR OTHER INFORMATION	PHONE NO./EMAIL:
		SIGNATURE OF SIGNER
		X

RECORD NO. 98	DOCUMENT TYPE/DATE	NOTARIZATION TYPE: ACKNOWLEDGEMENT / JURAT / OTHER
DATE	ID INFORMATION OR CREDIBLE WITNESS	PRINTED NAME & ADDRESS OF SIGNER
TIME ☐ AM ☐ PM		
FEE	☐ PERSONAL KNOWLEDGE	
	☐ DL, PASSPORT OR OTHER ID CARD	
THUMBPRINT	☐ CREDIBLE WITNESS ID & SIGNATURE	
	ADDRESS OF NOTARY OR OTHER INFORMATION	PHONE NO./EMAIL:
		SIGNATURE OF SIGNER
		X

RECORD NO. 99	DOCUMENT TYPE/DATE	NOTARIZATION TYPE: ACKNOWLEDGEMENT / JURAT / OTHER
DATE	ID INFORMATION OR CREDIBLE WITNESS	PRINTED NAME & ADDRESS OF SIGNER
TIME ☐ AM ☐ PM		
FEE	☐ PERSONAL KNOWLEDGE	
	☐ DL, PASSPORT OR OTHER ID CARD	
THUMBPRINT	☐ CREDIBLE WITNESS ID & SIGNATURE	
	ADDRESS OF NOTARY OR OTHER INFORMATION	PHONE NO./EMAIL:
		SIGNATURE OF SIGNER
		X

DOCUMENT TYPE/DATE	NOTARIZATION TYPE: ACKNOWLEDGEMENT / JURAT / OTHER	RECORD NO. 100

DATE	ID INFORMATION OR CREDIBLE WITNESS	PRINTED NAME & ADDRESS OF SIGNER
TIME ☐ AM ☐ PM		
FEE	☐ PERSONAL KNOWLEDGE	
THUMBPRINT	☐ DL, PASSPORT OR OTHER ID CARD	
	☐ CREDIBLE WITNESS ID & SIGNATURE	
	ADDRESS OF NOTARY OR OTHER INFORMATION	PHONE NO./EMAIL:
		SIGNATURE OF SIGNER
		X

DOCUMENT TYPE/DATE	NOTARIZATION TYPE: ACKNOWLEDGEMENT / JURAT / OTHER	RECORD NO. 101

DATE	ID INFORMATION OR CREDIBLE WITNESS	PRINTED NAME & ADDRESS OF SIGNER
TIME ☐ AM ☐ PM		
FEE	☐ PERSONAL KNOWLEDGE	
THUMBPRINT	☐ DL, PASSPORT OR OTHER ID CARD	
	☐ CREDIBLE WITNESS ID & SIGNATURE	
	ADDRESS OF NOTARY OR OTHER INFORMATION	PHONE NO./EMAIL:
		SIGNATURE OF SIGNER
		X

DOCUMENT TYPE/DATE	NOTARIZATION TYPE: ACKNOWLEDGEMENT / JURAT / OTHER	RECORD NO. 102

DATE	ID INFORMATION OR CREDIBLE WITNESS	PRINTED NAME & ADDRESS OF SIGNER
TIME ☐ AM ☐ PM		
FEE	☐ PERSONAL KNOWLEDGE	
THUMBPRINT	☐ DL, PASSPORT OR OTHER ID CARD	
	☐ CREDIBLE WITNESS ID & SIGNATURE	
	ADDRESS OF NOTARY OR OTHER INFORMATION	PHONE NO./EMAIL:
		SIGNATURE OF SIGNER
		X

RECORD NO. 103	DOCUMENT TYPE/DATE	NOTARIZATION TYPE: ACKNOWLEDGEMENT / JURAT / OTHER
DATE	ID INFORMATION OR CREDIBLE WITNESS	PRINTED NAME & ADDRESS OF SIGNER
TIME ☐ AM ☐ PM		
FEE	☐ PERSONAL KNOWLEDGE ☐ DL, PASSPORT OR OTHER ID CARD ☐ CREDIBLE WITNESS ID & SIGNATURE	
THUMBPRINT		
	ADDRESS OF NOTARY OR OTHER INFORMATION	PHONE NO./EMAIL:
		SIGNATURE OF SIGNER
		X

RECORD NO. 104	DOCUMENT TYPE/DATE	NOTARIZATION TYPE: ACKNOWLEDGEMENT / JURAT / OTHER
DATE	ID INFORMATION OR CREDIBLE WITNESS	PRINTED NAME & ADDRESS OF SIGNER
TIME ☐ AM ☐ PM		
FEE	☐ PERSONAL KNOWLEDGE ☐ DL, PASSPORT OR OTHER ID CARD ☐ CREDIBLE WITNESS ID & SIGNATURE	
THUMBPRINT		
	ADDRESS OF NOTARY OR OTHER INFORMATION	PHONE NO./EMAIL:
		SIGNATURE OF SIGNER
		X

RECORD NO. 105	DOCUMENT TYPE/DATE	NOTARIZATION TYPE: ACKNOWLEDGEMENT / JURAT / OTHER
DATE	ID INFORMATION OR CREDIBLE WITNESS	PRINTED NAME & ADDRESS OF SIGNER
TIME ☐ AM ☐ PM		
FEE	☐ PERSONAL KNOWLEDGE ☐ DL, PASSPORT OR OTHER ID CARD ☐ CREDIBLE WITNESS ID & SIGNATURE	
THUMBPRINT		
	ADDRESS OF NOTARY OR OTHER INFORMATION	PHONE NO./EMAIL:
		SIGNATURE OF SIGNER
		X

| DOCUMENT TYPE/DATE | NOTARIZATION TYPE: ACKNOWLEDGEMENT / JURAT / OTHER | RECORD NO. 106 |

| DATE | ID INFORMATION OR CREDIBLE WITNESS | PRINTED NAME & ADDRESS OF SIGNER |

TIME ☐ AM ☐ PM

FEE

☐ PERSONAL KNOWLEDGE
☐ DL, PASSPORT OR OTHER ID CARD
☐ CREDIBLE WITNESS ID & SIGNATURE

THUMBPRINT

| ADDRESS OF NOTARY OR OTHER INFORMATION | PHONE NO./EMAIL: |

SIGNATURE OF SIGNER

X

| DOCUMENT TYPE/DATE | NOTARIZATION TYPE: ACKNOWLEDGEMENT / JURAT / OTHER | RECORD NO. 107 |

| DATE | ID INFORMATION OR CREDIBLE WITNESS | PRINTED NAME & ADDRESS OF SIGNER |

TIME ☐ AM ☐ PM

FEE

☐ PERSONAL KNOWLEDGE
☐ DL, PASSPORT OR OTHER ID CARD
☐ CREDIBLE WITNESS ID & SIGNATURE

THUMBPRINT

| ADDRESS OF NOTARY OR OTHER INFORMATION | PHONE NO./EMAIL: |

SIGNATURE OF SIGNER

X

| DOCUMENT TYPE/DATE | NOTARIZATION TYPE: ACKNOWLEDGEMENT / JURAT / OTHER | RECORD NO. 108 |

| DATE | ID INFORMATION OR CREDIBLE WITNESS | PRINTED NAME & ADDRESS OF SIGNER |

TIME ☐ AM ☐ PM

FEE

☐ PERSONAL KNOWLEDGE
☐ DL, PASSPORT OR OTHER ID CARD
☐ CREDIBLE WITNESS ID & SIGNATURE

THUMBPRINT

| ADDRESS OF NOTARY OR OTHER INFORMATION | PHONE NO./EMAIL: |

SIGNATURE OF SIGNER

X

RECORD NO. 109	DOCUMENT TYPE/DATE	NOTARIZATION TYPE: ACKNOWLEDGEMENT / JURAT / OTHER
DATE	ID INFORMATION OR CREDIBLE WITNESS	PRINTED NAME & ADDRESS OF SIGNER
TIME ☐ AM ☐ PM		
FEE	☐ PERSONAL KNOWLEDGE	
THUMBPRINT	☐ DL, PASSPORT OR OTHER ID CARD ☐ CREDIBLE WITNESS ID & SIGNATURE	
	ADDRESS OF NOTARY OR OTHER INFORMATION	PHONE NO./EMAIL:
		SIGNATURE OF SIGNER X

RECORD NO. 110	DOCUMENT TYPE/DATE	NOTARIZATION TYPE: ACKNOWLEDGEMENT / JURAT / OTHER
DATE	ID INFORMATION OR CREDIBLE WITNESS	PRINTED NAME & ADDRESS OF SIGNER
TIME ☐ AM ☐ PM		
FEE	☐ PERSONAL KNOWLEDGE	
THUMBPRINT	☐ DL, PASSPORT OR OTHER ID CARD ☐ CREDIBLE WITNESS ID & SIGNATURE	
	ADDRESS OF NOTARY OR OTHER INFORMATION	PHONE NO./EMAIL:
		SIGNATURE OF SIGNER X

RECORD NO. 111	DOCUMENT TYPE/DATE	NOTARIZATION TYPE: ACKNOWLEDGEMENT / JURAT / OTHER
DATE	ID INFORMATION OR CREDIBLE WITNESS	PRINTED NAME & ADDRESS OF SIGNER
TIME ☐ AM ☐ PM		
FEE	☐ PERSONAL KNOWLEDGE	
THUMBPRINT	☐ DL, PASSPORT OR OTHER ID CARD ☐ CREDIBLE WITNESS ID & SIGNATURE	
	ADDRESS OF NOTARY OR OTHER INFORMATION	PHONE NO./EMAIL:
		SIGNATURE OF SIGNER X

DOCUMENT TYPE/DATE	NOTARIZATION TYPE: ACKNOWLEDGEMENT / JURAT / OTHER	RECORD NO. 112

DATE	ID INFORMATION OR CREDIBLE WITNESS	PRINTED NAME & ADDRESS OF SIGNER
TIME ☐ AM ☐ PM		
FEE	☐ PERSONAL KNOWLEDGE	
	☐ DL, PASSPORT OR OTHER ID CARD	
THUMBPRINT	☐ CREDIBLE WITNESS ID & SIGNATURE	

ADDRESS OF NOTARY OR OTHER INFORMATION	PHONE NO./EMAIL:
	SIGNATURE OF SIGNER
	X

DOCUMENT TYPE/DATE	NOTARIZATION TYPE: ACKNOWLEDGEMENT / JURAT / OTHER	RECORD NO. 113

DATE	ID INFORMATION OR CREDIBLE WITNESS	PRINTED NAME & ADDRESS OF SIGNER
TIME ☐ AM ☐ PM		
FEE	☐ PERSONAL KNOWLEDGE	
	☐ DL, PASSPORT OR OTHER ID CARD	
THUMBPRINT	☐ CREDIBLE WITNESS ID & SIGNATURE	

ADDRESS OF NOTARY OR OTHER INFORMATION	PHONE NO./EMAIL:
	SIGNATURE OF SIGNER
	X

DOCUMENT TYPE/DATE	NOTARIZATION TYPE: ACKNOWLEDGEMENT / JURAT / OTHER	RECORD NO. 114

DATE	ID INFORMATION OR CREDIBLE WITNESS	PRINTED NAME & ADDRESS OF SIGNER
TIME ☐ AM ☐ PM		
FEE	☐ PERSONAL KNOWLEDGE	
	☐ DL, PASSPORT OR OTHER ID CARD	
THUMBPRINT	☐ CREDIBLE WITNESS ID & SIGNATURE	

ADDRESS OF NOTARY OR OTHER INFORMATION	PHONE NO./EMAIL:
	SIGNATURE OF SIGNER
	X

RECORD NO. 115	DOCUMENT TYPE/DATE	NOTARIZATION TYPE: ACKNOWLEDGEMENT / JURAT / OTHER
DATE	ID INFORMATION OR CREDIBLE WITNESS	PRINTED NAME & ADDRESS OF SIGNER
TIME ☐ AM ☐ PM		
FEE	☐ PERSONAL KNOWLEDGE ☐ DL, PASSPORT OR OTHER ID CARD ☐ CREDIBLE WITNESS ID & SIGNATURE	
THUMBPRINT	ADDRESS OF NOTARY OR OTHER INFORMATION	PHONE NO./EMAIL:
		SIGNATURE OF SIGNER X

RECORD NO. 116	DOCUMENT TYPE/DATE	NOTARIZATION TYPE: ACKNOWLEDGEMENT / JURAT / OTHER
DATE	ID INFORMATION OR CREDIBLE WITNESS	PRINTED NAME & ADDRESS OF SIGNER
TIME ☐ AM ☐ PM		
FEE	☐ PERSONAL KNOWLEDGE ☐ DL, PASSPORT OR OTHER ID CARD ☐ CREDIBLE WITNESS ID & SIGNATURE	
THUMBPRINT	ADDRESS OF NOTARY OR OTHER INFORMATION	PHONE NO./EMAIL:
		SIGNATURE OF SIGNER X

RECORD NO. 117	DOCUMENT TYPE/DATE	NOTARIZATION TYPE: ACKNOWLEDGEMENT / JURAT / OTHER
DATE	ID INFORMATION OR CREDIBLE WITNESS	PRINTED NAME & ADDRESS OF SIGNER
TIME ☐ AM ☐ PM		
FEE	☐ PERSONAL KNOWLEDGE ☐ DL, PASSPORT OR OTHER ID CARD ☐ CREDIBLE WITNESS ID & SIGNATURE	
THUMBPRINT	ADDRESS OF NOTARY OR OTHER INFORMATION	PHONE NO./EMAIL:
		SIGNATURE OF SIGNER X

DOCUMENT TYPE/DATE	NOTARIZATION TYPE: ACKNOWLEDGEMENT / JURAT / OTHER	RECORD NO. 118

DATE	ID INFORMATION OR CREDIBLE WITNESS	PRINTED NAME & ADDRESS OF SIGNER
TIME ☐ AM ☐ PM		
FEE	☐ PERSONAL KNOWLEDGE	
THUMBPRINT	☐ DL, PASSPORT OR OTHER ID CARD ☐ CREDIBLE WITNESS ID & SIGNATURE	
	ADDRESS OF NOTARY OR OTHER INFORMATION	PHONE NO./EMAIL:
		SIGNATURE OF SIGNER X

DOCUMENT TYPE/DATE	NOTARIZATION TYPE: ACKNOWLEDGEMENT / JURAT / OTHER	RECORD NO. 119

DATE	ID INFORMATION OR CREDIBLE WITNESS	PRINTED NAME & ADDRESS OF SIGNER
TIME ☐ AM ☐ PM		
FEE	☐ PERSONAL KNOWLEDGE	
THUMBPRINT	☐ DL, PASSPORT OR OTHER ID CARD ☐ CREDIBLE WITNESS ID & SIGNATURE	
	ADDRESS OF NOTARY OR OTHER INFORMATION	PHONE NO./EMAIL:
		SIGNATURE OF SIGNER X

DOCUMENT TYPE/DATE	NOTARIZATION TYPE: ACKNOWLEDGEMENT / JURAT / OTHER	RECORD NO. 120

DATE	ID INFORMATION OR CREDIBLE WITNESS	PRINTED NAME & ADDRESS OF SIGNER
TIME ☐ AM ☐ PM		
FEE	☐ PERSONAL KNOWLEDGE	
THUMBPRINT	☐ DL, PASSPORT OR OTHER ID CARD ☐ CREDIBLE WITNESS ID & SIGNATURE	
	ADDRESS OF NOTARY OR OTHER INFORMATION	PHONE NO./EMAIL:
		SIGNATURE OF SIGNER X

RECORD NO. 121	DOCUMENT TYPE/DATE	NOTARIZATION TYPE: ACKNOWLEDGEMENT / JURAT / OTHER
DATE	ID INFORMATION OR CREDIBLE WITNESS	PRINTED NAME & ADDRESS OF SIGNER
TIME ☐ AM ☐ PM		
FEE	☐ PERSONAL KNOWLEDGE	
	☐ DL, PASSPORT OR OTHER ID CARD	
THUMBPRINT	☐ CREDIBLE WITNESS ID & SIGNATURE	
	ADDRESS OF NOTARY OR OTHER INFORMATION	PHONE NO./EMAIL:
		SIGNATURE OF SIGNER
		X

RECORD NO. 122	DOCUMENT TYPE/DATE	NOTARIZATION TYPE: ACKNOWLEDGEMENT / JURAT / OTHER
DATE	ID INFORMATION OR CREDIBLE WITNESS	PRINTED NAME & ADDRESS OF SIGNER
TIME ☐ AM ☐ PM		
FEE	☐ PERSONAL KNOWLEDGE	
	☐ DL, PASSPORT OR OTHER ID CARD	
THUMBPRINT	☐ CREDIBLE WITNESS ID & SIGNATURE	
	ADDRESS OF NOTARY OR OTHER INFORMATION	PHONE NO./EMAIL:
		SIGNATURE OF SIGNER
		X

RECORD NO. 123	DOCUMENT TYPE/DATE	NOTARIZATION TYPE: ACKNOWLEDGEMENT / JURAT / OTHER
DATE	ID INFORMATION OR CREDIBLE WITNESS	PRINTED NAME & ADDRESS OF SIGNER
TIME ☐ AM ☐ PM		
FEE	☐ PERSONAL KNOWLEDGE	
	☐ DL, PASSPORT OR OTHER ID CARD	
THUMBPRINT	☐ CREDIBLE WITNESS ID & SIGNATURE	
	ADDRESS OF NOTARY OR OTHER INFORMATION	PHONE NO./EMAIL:
		SIGNATURE OF SIGNER
		X

DOCUMENT TYPE/DATE	NOTARIZATION TYPE: ACKNOWLEDGEMENT / JURAT / OTHER	RECORD NO. 124

DATE	ID INFORMATION OR CREDIBLE WITNESS	PRINTED NAME & ADDRESS OF SIGNER
TIME ☐ AM ☐ PM		
FEE	☐ PERSONAL KNOWLEDGE	
	☐ DL, PASSPORT OR OTHER ID CARD	
THUMBPRINT	☐ CREDIBLE WITNESS ID & SIGNATURE	
	ADDRESS OF NOTARY OR OTHER INFORMATION	PHONE NO./EMAIL:
		SIGNATURE OF SIGNER
		X

DOCUMENT TYPE/DATE	NOTARIZATION TYPE: ACKNOWLEDGEMENT / JURAT / OTHER	RECORD NO. 125

DATE	ID INFORMATION OR CREDIBLE WITNESS	PRINTED NAME & ADDRESS OF SIGNER
TIME ☐ AM ☐ PM		
FEE	☐ PERSONAL KNOWLEDGE	
	☐ DL, PASSPORT OR OTHER ID CARD	
THUMBPRINT	☐ CREDIBLE WITNESS ID & SIGNATURE	
	ADDRESS OF NOTARY OR OTHER INFORMATION	PHONE NO./EMAIL:
		SIGNATURE OF SIGNER
		X

DOCUMENT TYPE/DATE	NOTARIZATION TYPE: ACKNOWLEDGEMENT / JURAT / OTHER	RECORD NO. 126

DATE	ID INFORMATION OR CREDIBLE WITNESS	PRINTED NAME & ADDRESS OF SIGNER
TIME ☐ AM ☐ PM		
FEE	☐ PERSONAL KNOWLEDGE	
	☐ DL, PASSPORT OR OTHER ID CARD	
THUMBPRINT	☐ CREDIBLE WITNESS ID & SIGNATURE	
	ADDRESS OF NOTARY OR OTHER INFORMATION	PHONE NO./EMAIL:
		SIGNATURE OF SIGNER
		X

RECORD NO. 127	DOCUMENT TYPE/DATE	NOTARIZATION TYPE: ACKNOWLEDGEMENT / JURAT / OTHER
DATE	ID INFORMATION OR CREDIBLE WITNESS	PRINTED NAME & ADDRESS OF SIGNER
TIME ☐ AM ☐ PM		
FEE	☐ PERSONAL KNOWLEDGE	
	☐ DL, PASSPORT OR OTHER ID CARD	
THUMBPRINT	☐ CREDIBLE WITNESS ID & SIGNATURE	
	ADDRESS OF NOTARY OR OTHER INFORMATION	PHONE NO./EMAIL:
		SIGNATURE OF SIGNER
		X

RECORD NO. 128	DOCUMENT TYPE/DATE	NOTARIZATION TYPE: ACKNOWLEDGEMENT / JURAT / OTHER
DATE	ID INFORMATION OR CREDIBLE WITNESS	PRINTED NAME & ADDRESS OF SIGNER
TIME ☐ AM ☐ PM		
FEE	☐ PERSONAL KNOWLEDGE	
	☐ DL, PASSPORT OR OTHER ID CARD	
THUMBPRINT	☐ CREDIBLE WITNESS ID & SIGNATURE	
	ADDRESS OF NOTARY OR OTHER INFORMATION	PHONE NO./EMAIL:
		SIGNATURE OF SIGNER
		X

RECORD NO. 129	DOCUMENT TYPE/DATE	NOTARIZATION TYPE: ACKNOWLEDGEMENT / JURAT / OTHER
DATE	ID INFORMATION OR CREDIBLE WITNESS	PRINTED NAME & ADDRESS OF SIGNER
TIME ☐ AM ☐ PM		
FEE	☐ PERSONAL KNOWLEDGE	
	☐ DL, PASSPORT OR OTHER ID CARD	
THUMBPRINT	☐ CREDIBLE WITNESS ID & SIGNATURE	
	ADDRESS OF NOTARY OR OTHER INFORMATION	PHONE NO./EMAIL:
		SIGNATURE OF SIGNER
		X

DOCUMENT TYPE/DATE	NOTARIZATION TYPE: ACKNOWLEDGEMENT / JURAT / OTHER	RECORD NO. 130

DATE	ID INFORMATION OR CREDIBLE WITNESS	PRINTED NAME & ADDRESS OF SIGNER
TIME ☐ AM ☐ PM		
FEE	☐ PERSONAL KNOWLEDGE	
THUMBPRINT	☐ DL, PASSPORT OR OTHER ID CARD ☐ CREDIBLE WITNESS ID & SIGNATURE	
	ADDRESS OF NOTARY OR OTHER INFORMATION	PHONE NO./EMAIL:
		SIGNATURE OF SIGNER X

DOCUMENT TYPE/DATE	NOTARIZATION TYPE: ACKNOWLEDGEMENT / JURAT / OTHER	RECORD NO. 131

DATE	ID INFORMATION OR CREDIBLE WITNESS	PRINTED NAME & ADDRESS OF SIGNER
TIME ☐ AM ☐ PM		
FEE	☐ PERSONAL KNOWLEDGE	
THUMBPRINT	☐ DL, PASSPORT OR OTHER ID CARD ☐ CREDIBLE WITNESS ID & SIGNATURE	
	ADDRESS OF NOTARY OR OTHER INFORMATION	PHONE NO./EMAIL:
		SIGNATURE OF SIGNER X

DOCUMENT TYPE/DATE	NOTARIZATION TYPE: ACKNOWLEDGEMENT / JURAT / OTHER	RECORD NO. 132

DATE	ID INFORMATION OR CREDIBLE WITNESS	PRINTED NAME & ADDRESS OF SIGNER
TIME ☐ AM ☐ PM		
FEE	☐ PERSONAL KNOWLEDGE	
THUMBPRINT	☐ DL, PASSPORT OR OTHER ID CARD ☐ CREDIBLE WITNESS ID & SIGNATURE	
	ADDRESS OF NOTARY OR OTHER INFORMATION	PHONE NO./EMAIL:
		SIGNATURE OF SIGNER X

RECORD NO.	DOCUMENT TYPE/DATE	NOTARIZATION TYPE: ACKNOWLEDGEMENT / JURAT / OTHER
133		
DATE	ID INFORMATION OR CREDIBLE WITNESS	PRINTED NAME & ADDRESS OF SIGNER
TIME ☐ AM ☐ PM		
FEE	☐ PERSONAL KNOWLEDGE	
	☐ DL, PASSPORT OR OTHER ID CARD	
THUMBPRINT	☐ CREDIBLE WITNESS ID & SIGNATURE	
	ADDRESS OF NOTARY OR OTHER INFORMATION	PHONE NO./EMAIL:
		SIGNATURE OF SIGNER
		X

RECORD NO.	DOCUMENT TYPE/DATE	NOTARIZATION TYPE: ACKNOWLEDGEMENT / JURAT / OTHER
134		
DATE	ID INFORMATION OR CREDIBLE WITNESS	PRINTED NAME & ADDRESS OF SIGNER
TIME ☐ AM ☐ PM		
FEE	☐ PERSONAL KNOWLEDGE	
	☐ DL, PASSPORT OR OTHER ID CARD	
THUMBPRINT	☐ CREDIBLE WITNESS ID & SIGNATURE	
	ADDRESS OF NOTARY OR OTHER INFORMATION	PHONE NO./EMAIL:
		SIGNATURE OF SIGNER
		X

RECORD NO.	DOCUMENT TYPE/DATE	NOTARIZATION TYPE: ACKNOWLEDGEMENT / JURAT / OTHER
135		
DATE	ID INFORMATION OR CREDIBLE WITNESS	PRINTED NAME & ADDRESS OF SIGNER
TIME ☐ AM ☐ PM		
FEE	☐ PERSONAL KNOWLEDGE	
	☐ DL, PASSPORT OR OTHER ID CARD	
THUMBPRINT	☐ CREDIBLE WITNESS ID & SIGNATURE	
	ADDRESS OF NOTARY OR OTHER INFORMATION	PHONE NO./EMAIL:
		SIGNATURE OF SIGNER
		X

DOCUMENT TYPE/DATE	NOTARIZATION TYPE: ACKNOWLEDGEMENT / JURAT / OTHER	RECORD NO. 136

DATE	ID INFORMATION OR CREDIBLE WITNESS	PRINTED NAME & ADDRESS OF SIGNER
TIME ☐ AM ☐ PM		
FEE	☐ PERSONAL KNOWLEDGE	
THUMBPRINT	☐ DL, PASSPORT OR OTHER ID CARD	
	☐ CREDIBLE WITNESS ID & SIGNATURE	
	ADDRESS OF NOTARY OR OTHER INFORMATION	PHONE NO./EMAIL:
		SIGNATURE OF SIGNER
		X

DOCUMENT TYPE/DATE	NOTARIZATION TYPE: ACKNOWLEDGEMENT / JURAT / OTHER	RECORD NO. 137

DATE	ID INFORMATION OR CREDIBLE WITNESS	PRINTED NAME & ADDRESS OF SIGNER
TIME ☐ AM ☐ PM		
FEE	☐ PERSONAL KNOWLEDGE	
THUMBPRINT	☐ DL, PASSPORT OR OTHER ID CARD	
	☐ CREDIBLE WITNESS ID & SIGNATURE	
	ADDRESS OF NOTARY OR OTHER INFORMATION	PHONE NO./EMAIL:
		SIGNATURE OF SIGNER
		X

DOCUMENT TYPE/DATE	NOTARIZATION TYPE: ACKNOWLEDGEMENT / JURAT / OTHER	RECORD NO. 138

DATE	ID INFORMATION OR CREDIBLE WITNESS	PRINTED NAME & ADDRESS OF SIGNER
TIME ☐ AM ☐ PM		
FEE	☐ PERSONAL KNOWLEDGE	
THUMBPRINT	☐ DL, PASSPORT OR OTHER ID CARD	
	☐ CREDIBLE WITNESS ID & SIGNATURE	
	ADDRESS OF NOTARY OR OTHER INFORMATION	PHONE NO./EMAIL:
		SIGNATURE OF SIGNER
		X

RECORD NO. 139	DOCUMENT TYPE/DATE	NOTARIZATION TYPE: ACKNOWLEDGEMENT / JURAT / OTHER
DATE	ID INFORMATION OR CREDIBLE WITNESS	PRINTED NAME & ADDRESS OF SIGNER
TIME ☐ AM ☐ PM		
FEE	☐ PERSONAL KNOWLEDGE	
	☐ DL, PASSPORT OR OTHER ID CARD	
THUMBPRINT	☐ CREDIBLE WITNESS ID & SIGNATURE	
	ADDRESS OF NOTARY OR OTHER INFORMATION	PHONE NO./EMAIL:
		SIGNATURE OF SIGNER
		X

RECORD NO. 140	DOCUMENT TYPE/DATE	NOTARIZATION TYPE: ACKNOWLEDGEMENT / JURAT / OTHER
DATE	ID INFORMATION OR CREDIBLE WITNESS	PRINTED NAME & ADDRESS OF SIGNER
TIME ☐ AM ☐ PM		
FEE	☐ PERSONAL KNOWLEDGE	
	☐ DL, PASSPORT OR OTHER ID CARD	
THUMBPRINT	☐ CREDIBLE WITNESS ID & SIGNATURE	
	ADDRESS OF NOTARY OR OTHER INFORMATION	PHONE NO./EMAIL:
		SIGNATURE OF SIGNER
		X

RECORD NO. 141	DOCUMENT TYPE/DATE	NOTARIZATION TYPE: ACKNOWLEDGEMENT / JURAT / OTHER
DATE	ID INFORMATION OR CREDIBLE WITNESS	PRINTED NAME & ADDRESS OF SIGNER
TIME ☐ AM ☐ PM		
FEE	☐ PERSONAL KNOWLEDGE	
	☐ DL, PASSPORT OR OTHER ID CARD	
THUMBPRINT	☐ CREDIBLE WITNESS ID & SIGNATURE	
	ADDRESS OF NOTARY OR OTHER INFORMATION	PHONE NO./EMAIL:
		SIGNATURE OF SIGNER
		X

DOCUMENT TYPE/DATE	NOTARIZATION TYPE: ACKNOWLEDGEMENT / JURAT / OTHER	RECORD NO. 142

DATE	ID INFORMATION OR CREDIBLE WITNESS	PRINTED NAME & ADDRESS OF SIGNER
TIME ☐ AM ☐ PM		
FEE	☐ PERSONAL KNOWLEDGE	
	☐ DL, PASSPORT OR OTHER ID CARD	
THUMBPRINT	☐ CREDIBLE WITNESS ID & SIGNATURE	
	ADDRESS OF NOTARY OR OTHER INFORMATION	PHONE NO./EMAIL:
		SIGNATURE OF SIGNER
		X

DOCUMENT TYPE/DATE	NOTARIZATION TYPE: ACKNOWLEDGEMENT / JURAT / OTHER	RECORD NO. 143

DATE	ID INFORMATION OR CREDIBLE WITNESS	PRINTED NAME & ADDRESS OF SIGNER
TIME ☐ AM ☐ PM		
FEE	☐ PERSONAL KNOWLEDGE	
	☐ DL, PASSPORT OR OTHER ID CARD	
THUMBPRINT	☐ CREDIBLE WITNESS ID & SIGNATURE	
	ADDRESS OF NOTARY OR OTHER INFORMATION	PHONE NO./EMAIL:
		SIGNATURE OF SIGNER
		X

DOCUMENT TYPE/DATE	NOTARIZATION TYPE: ACKNOWLEDGEMENT / JURAT / OTHER	RECORD NO. 144

DATE	ID INFORMATION OR CREDIBLE WITNESS	PRINTED NAME & ADDRESS OF SIGNER
TIME ☐ AM ☐ PM		
FEE	☐ PERSONAL KNOWLEDGE	
	☐ DL, PASSPORT OR OTHER ID CARD	
THUMBPRINT	☐ CREDIBLE WITNESS ID & SIGNATURE	
	ADDRESS OF NOTARY OR OTHER INFORMATION	PHONE NO./EMAIL:
		SIGNATURE OF SIGNER
		X

RECORD NO. 145	DOCUMENT TYPE/DATE	NOTARIZATION TYPE: ACKNOWLEDGEMENT / JURAT / OTHER
DATE **TIME** ☐ AM ☐ PM **FEE** **THUMBPRINT**	ID INFORMATION OR CREDIBLE WITNESS ☐ PERSONAL KNOWLEDGE ☐ DL, PASSPORT OR OTHER ID CARD ☐ CREDIBLE WITNESS ID & SIGNATURE	PRINTED NAME & ADDRESS OF SIGNER
	ADDRESS OF NOTARY OR OTHER INFORMATION	PHONE NO./EMAIL:
		SIGNATURE OF SIGNER X

RECORD NO. 146	DOCUMENT TYPE/DATE	NOTARIZATION TYPE: ACKNOWLEDGEMENT / JURAT / OTHER
DATE **TIME** ☐ AM ☐ PM **FEE** **THUMBPRINT**	ID INFORMATION OR CREDIBLE WITNESS ☐ PERSONAL KNOWLEDGE ☐ DL, PASSPORT OR OTHER ID CARD ☐ CREDIBLE WITNESS ID & SIGNATURE	PRINTED NAME & ADDRESS OF SIGNER
	ADDRESS OF NOTARY OR OTHER INFORMATION	PHONE NO./EMAIL:
		SIGNATURE OF SIGNER X

RECORD NO. 147	DOCUMENT TYPE/DATE	NOTARIZATION TYPE: ACKNOWLEDGEMENT / JURAT / OTHER
DATE **TIME** ☐ AM ☐ PM **FEE** **THUMBPRINT**	ID INFORMATION OR CREDIBLE WITNESS ☐ PERSONAL KNOWLEDGE ☐ DL, PASSPORT OR OTHER ID CARD ☐ CREDIBLE WITNESS ID & SIGNATURE	PRINTED NAME & ADDRESS OF SIGNER
	ADDRESS OF NOTARY OR OTHER INFORMATION	PHONE NO./EMAIL:
		SIGNATURE OF SIGNER X

DOCUMENT TYPE/DATE	NOTARIZATION TYPE: ACKNOWLEDGEMENT / JURAT / OTHER	RECORD NO. 148

DATE	ID INFORMATION OR CREDIBLE WITNESS	PRINTED NAME & ADDRESS OF SIGNER
TIME ☐ AM ☐ PM		
FEE	☐ PERSONAL KNOWLEDGE	
	☐ DL, PASSPORT OR OTHER ID CARD	
THUMBPRINT	☐ CREDIBLE WITNESS ID & SIGNATURE	

ADDRESS OF NOTARY OR OTHER INFORMATION	PHONE NO./EMAIL:
	SIGNATURE OF SIGNER
	X

DOCUMENT TYPE/DATE	NOTARIZATION TYPE: ACKNOWLEDGEMENT / JURAT / OTHER	RECORD NO. 149

DATE	ID INFORMATION OR CREDIBLE WITNESS	PRINTED NAME & ADDRESS OF SIGNER
TIME ☐ AM ☐ PM		
FEE	☐ PERSONAL KNOWLEDGE	
	☐ DL, PASSPORT OR OTHER ID CARD	
THUMBPRINT	☐ CREDIBLE WITNESS ID & SIGNATURE	

ADDRESS OF NOTARY OR OTHER INFORMATION	PHONE NO./EMAIL:
	SIGNATURE OF SIGNER
	X

DOCUMENT TYPE/DATE	NOTARIZATION TYPE: ACKNOWLEDGEMENT / JURAT / OTHER	RECORD NO. 150

DATE	ID INFORMATION OR CREDIBLE WITNESS	PRINTED NAME & ADDRESS OF SIGNER
TIME ☐ AM ☐ PM		
FEE	☐ PERSONAL KNOWLEDGE	
	☐ DL, PASSPORT OR OTHER ID CARD	
THUMBPRINT	☐ CREDIBLE WITNESS ID & SIGNATURE	

ADDRESS OF NOTARY OR OTHER INFORMATION	PHONE NO./EMAIL:
	SIGNATURE OF SIGNER
	X

RECORD NO. 151	DOCUMENT TYPE/DATE	NOTARIZATION TYPE: ACKNOWLEDGEMENT / JURAT / OTHER
DATE	ID INFORMATION OR CREDIBLE WITNESS	PRINTED NAME & ADDRESS OF SIGNER
TIME ☐ AM ☐ PM		
FEE	☐ PERSONAL KNOWLEDGE	
THUMBPRINT	☐ DL, PASSPORT OR OTHER ID CARD ☐ CREDIBLE WITNESS ID & SIGNATURE	
	ADDRESS OF NOTARY OR OTHER INFORMATION	PHONE NO./EMAIL:
		SIGNATURE OF SIGNER
		X

RECORD NO. 152	DOCUMENT TYPE/DATE	NOTARIZATION TYPE: ACKNOWLEDGEMENT / JURAT / OTHER
DATE	ID INFORMATION OR CREDIBLE WITNESS	PRINTED NAME & ADDRESS OF SIGNER
TIME ☐ AM ☐ PM		
FEE	☐ PERSONAL KNOWLEDGE	
THUMBPRINT	☐ DL, PASSPORT OR OTHER ID CARD ☐ CREDIBLE WITNESS ID & SIGNATURE	
	ADDRESS OF NOTARY OR OTHER INFORMATION	PHONE NO./EMAIL:
		SIGNATURE OF SIGNER
		X

RECORD NO. 153	DOCUMENT TYPE/DATE	NOTARIZATION TYPE: ACKNOWLEDGEMENT / JURAT / OTHER
DATE	ID INFORMATION OR CREDIBLE WITNESS	PRINTED NAME & ADDRESS OF SIGNER
TIME ☐ AM ☐ PM		
FEE	☐ PERSONAL KNOWLEDGE	
THUMBPRINT	☐ DL, PASSPORT OR OTHER ID CARD ☐ CREDIBLE WITNESS ID & SIGNATURE	
	ADDRESS OF NOTARY OR OTHER INFORMATION	PHONE NO./EMAIL:
		SIGNATURE OF SIGNER
		X

DOCUMENT TYPE/DATE	NOTARIZATION TYPE: ACKNOWLEDGEMENT / JURAT / OTHER	RECORD NO. 154

DATE	ID INFORMATION OR CREDIBLE WITNESS	PRINTED NAME & ADDRESS OF SIGNER
TIME ☐ AM ☐ PM		
FEE	☐ PERSONAL KNOWLEDGE	
	☐ DL, PASSPORT OR OTHER ID CARD	
THUMBPRINT	☐ CREDIBLE WITNESS ID & SIGNATURE	
	ADDRESS OF NOTARY OR OTHER INFORMATION	PHONE NO./EMAIL:
		SIGNATURE OF SIGNER
		X

DOCUMENT TYPE/DATE	NOTARIZATION TYPE: ACKNOWLEDGEMENT / JURAT / OTHER	RECORD NO. 155

DATE	ID INFORMATION OR CREDIBLE WITNESS	PRINTED NAME & ADDRESS OF SIGNER
TIME ☐ AM ☐ PM		
FEE	☐ PERSONAL KNOWLEDGE	
	☐ DL, PASSPORT OR OTHER ID CARD	
THUMBPRINT	☐ CREDIBLE WITNESS ID & SIGNATURE	
	ADDRESS OF NOTARY OR OTHER INFORMATION	PHONE NO./EMAIL:
		SIGNATURE OF SIGNER
		X

DOCUMENT TYPE/DATE	NOTARIZATION TYPE: ACKNOWLEDGEMENT / JURAT / OTHER	RECORD NO. 156

DATE	ID INFORMATION OR CREDIBLE WITNESS	PRINTED NAME & ADDRESS OF SIGNER
TIME ☐ AM ☐ PM		
FEE	☐ PERSONAL KNOWLEDGE	
	☐ DL, PASSPORT OR OTHER ID CARD	
THUMBPRINT	☐ CREDIBLE WITNESS ID & SIGNATURE	
	ADDRESS OF NOTARY OR OTHER INFORMATION	PHONE NO./EMAIL:
		SIGNATURE OF SIGNER
		X

RECORD NO. 157	DOCUMENT TYPE/DATE	NOTARIZATION TYPE: ACKNOWLEDGEMENT / JURAT / OTHER
DATE	ID INFORMATION OR CREDIBLE WITNESS	PRINTED NAME & ADDRESS OF SIGNER
TIME ☐ AM ☐ PM		
FEE	☐ PERSONAL KNOWLEDGE	
	☐ DL, PASSPORT OR OTHER ID CARD	
THUMBPRINT	☐ CREDIBLE WITNESS ID & SIGNATURE	
	ADDRESS OF NOTARY OR OTHER INFORMATION	PHONE NO./EMAIL:
		SIGNATURE OF SIGNER
		X

RECORD NO. 158	DOCUMENT TYPE/DATE	NOTARIZATION TYPE: ACKNOWLEDGEMENT / JURAT / OTHER
DATE	ID INFORMATION OR CREDIBLE WITNESS	PRINTED NAME & ADDRESS OF SIGNER
TIME ☐ AM ☐ PM		
FEE	☐ PERSONAL KNOWLEDGE	
	☐ DL, PASSPORT OR OTHER ID CARD	
THUMBPRINT	☐ CREDIBLE WITNESS ID & SIGNATURE	
	ADDRESS OF NOTARY OR OTHER INFORMATION	PHONE NO./EMAIL:
		SIGNATURE OF SIGNER
		X

RECORD NO. 159	DOCUMENT TYPE/DATE	NOTARIZATION TYPE: ACKNOWLEDGEMENT / JURAT / OTHER
DATE	ID INFORMATION OR CREDIBLE WITNESS	PRINTED NAME & ADDRESS OF SIGNER
TIME ☐ AM ☐ PM		
FEE	☐ PERSONAL KNOWLEDGE	
	☐ DL, PASSPORT OR OTHER ID CARD	
THUMBPRINT	☐ CREDIBLE WITNESS ID & SIGNATURE	
	ADDRESS OF NOTARY OR OTHER INFORMATION	PHONE NO./EMAIL:
		SIGNATURE OF SIGNER
		X

DOCUMENT TYPE/DATE	NOTARIZATION TYPE: ACKNOWLEDGEMENT / JURAT / OTHER	RECORD NO. 154

DATE	ID INFORMATION OR CREDIBLE WITNESS	PRINTED NAME & ADDRESS OF SIGNER
TIME ☐ AM ☐ PM		
FEE	☐ PERSONAL KNOWLEDGE ☐ DL, PASSPORT OR OTHER ID CARD ☐ CREDIBLE WITNESS ID & SIGNATURE	
THUMBPRINT	ADDRESS OF NOTARY OR OTHER INFORMATION	PHONE NO./EMAIL:
		SIGNATURE OF SIGNER X

DOCUMENT TYPE/DATE	NOTARIZATION TYPE: ACKNOWLEDGEMENT / JURAT / OTHER	RECORD NO. 155

DATE	ID INFORMATION OR CREDIBLE WITNESS	PRINTED NAME & ADDRESS OF SIGNER
TIME ☐ AM ☐ PM		
FEE	☐ PERSONAL KNOWLEDGE ☐ DL, PASSPORT OR OTHER ID CARD ☐ CREDIBLE WITNESS ID & SIGNATURE	
THUMBPRINT	ADDRESS OF NOTARY OR OTHER INFORMATION	PHONE NO./EMAIL:
		SIGNATURE OF SIGNER X

DOCUMENT TYPE/DATE	NOTARIZATION TYPE: ACKNOWLEDGEMENT / JURAT / OTHER	RECORD NO. 156

DATE	ID INFORMATION OR CREDIBLE WITNESS	PRINTED NAME & ADDRESS OF SIGNER
TIME ☐ AM ☐ PM		
FEE	☐ PERSONAL KNOWLEDGE ☐ DL, PASSPORT OR OTHER ID CARD ☐ CREDIBLE WITNESS ID & SIGNATURE	
THUMBPRINT	ADDRESS OF NOTARY OR OTHER INFORMATION	PHONE NO./EMAIL:
		SIGNATURE OF SIGNER X

RECORD NO. 157	DOCUMENT TYPE/DATE	NOTARIZATION TYPE: ACKNOWLEDGEMENT / JURAT / OTHER
DATE	ID INFORMATION OR CREDIBLE WITNESS	PRINTED NAME & ADDRESS OF SIGNER
TIME ☐ AM ☐ PM		
FEE	☐ PERSONAL KNOWLEDGE ☐ DL, PASSPORT OR OTHER ID CARD ☐ CREDIBLE WITNESS ID & SIGNATURE	
THUMBPRINT		
	ADDRESS OF NOTARY OR OTHER INFORMATION	PHONE NO./EMAIL:
		SIGNATURE OF SIGNER X

RECORD NO. 158	DOCUMENT TYPE/DATE	NOTARIZATION TYPE: ACKNOWLEDGEMENT / JURAT / OTHER
DATE	ID INFORMATION OR CREDIBLE WITNESS	PRINTED NAME & ADDRESS OF SIGNER
TIME ☐ AM ☐ PM		
FEE	☐ PERSONAL KNOWLEDGE ☐ DL, PASSPORT OR OTHER ID CARD ☐ CREDIBLE WITNESS ID & SIGNATURE	
THUMBPRINT		
	ADDRESS OF NOTARY OR OTHER INFORMATION	PHONE NO./EMAIL:
		SIGNATURE OF SIGNER X

RECORD NO. 159	DOCUMENT TYPE/DATE	NOTARIZATION TYPE: ACKNOWLEDGEMENT / JURAT / OTHER
DATE	ID INFORMATION OR CREDIBLE WITNESS	PRINTED NAME & ADDRESS OF SIGNER
TIME ☐ AM ☐ PM		
FEE	☐ PERSONAL KNOWLEDGE ☐ DL, PASSPORT OR OTHER ID CARD ☐ CREDIBLE WITNESS ID & SIGNATURE	
THUMBPRINT		
	ADDRESS OF NOTARY OR OTHER INFORMATION	PHONE NO./EMAIL:
		SIGNATURE OF SIGNER X

DOCUMENT TYPE/DATE	NOTARIZATION TYPE: ACKNOWLEDGEMENT / JURAT / OTHER	RECORD NO. 160

DATE	ID INFORMATION OR CREDIBLE WITNESS	PRINTED NAME & ADDRESS OF SIGNER
TIME ☐ AM ☐ PM		
FEE	☐ PERSONAL KNOWLEDGE	
THUMBPRINT	☐ DL, PASSPORT OR OTHER ID CARD ☐ CREDIBLE WITNESS ID & SIGNATURE	
	ADDRESS OF NOTARY OR OTHER INFORMATION	PHONE NO./EMAIL:
		SIGNATURE OF SIGNER
		X

DOCUMENT TYPE/DATE	NOTARIZATION TYPE: ACKNOWLEDGEMENT / JURAT / OTHER	RECORD NO. 161

DATE	ID INFORMATION OR CREDIBLE WITNESS	PRINTED NAME & ADDRESS OF SIGNER
TIME ☐ AM ☐ PM		
FEE	☐ PERSONAL KNOWLEDGE	
THUMBPRINT	☐ DL, PASSPORT OR OTHER ID CARD ☐ CREDIBLE WITNESS ID & SIGNATURE	
	ADDRESS OF NOTARY OR OTHER INFORMATION	PHONE NO./EMAIL:
		SIGNATURE OF SIGNER
		X

DOCUMENT TYPE/DATE	NOTARIZATION TYPE: ACKNOWLEDGEMENT / JURAT / OTHER	RECORD NO. 162

DATE	ID INFORMATION OR CREDIBLE WITNESS	PRINTED NAME & ADDRESS OF SIGNER
TIME ☐ AM ☐ PM		
FEE	☐ PERSONAL KNOWLEDGE	
THUMBPRINT	☐ DL, PASSPORT OR OTHER ID CARD ☐ CREDIBLE WITNESS ID & SIGNATURE	
	ADDRESS OF NOTARY OR OTHER INFORMATION	PHONE NO./EMAIL:
		SIGNATURE OF SIGNER
		X

RECORD NO. 163	DOCUMENT TYPE/DATE	NOTARIZATION TYPE: ACKNOWLEDGEMENT / JURAT / OTHER
DATE	ID INFORMATION OR CREDIBLE WITNESS	PRINTED NAME & ADDRESS OF SIGNER
TIME ☐ AM ☐ PM		
FEE	☐ PERSONAL KNOWLEDGE	
	☐ DL, PASSPORT OR OTHER ID CARD	
THUMBPRINT	☐ CREDIBLE WITNESS ID & SIGNATURE	
	ADDRESS OF NOTARY OR OTHER INFORMATION	PHONE NO./EMAIL:
		SIGNATURE OF SIGNER
		X

RECORD NO. 164	DOCUMENT TYPE/DATE	NOTARIZATION TYPE: ACKNOWLEDGEMENT / JURAT / OTHER
DATE	ID INFORMATION OR CREDIBLE WITNESS	PRINTED NAME & ADDRESS OF SIGNER
TIME ☐ AM ☐ PM		
FEE	☐ PERSONAL KNOWLEDGE	
	☐ DL, PASSPORT OR OTHER ID CARD	
THUMBPRINT	☐ CREDIBLE WITNESS ID & SIGNATURE	
	ADDRESS OF NOTARY OR OTHER INFORMATION	PHONE NO./EMAIL:
		SIGNATURE OF SIGNER
		X

RECORD NO. 165	DOCUMENT TYPE/DATE	NOTARIZATION TYPE: ACKNOWLEDGEMENT / JURAT / OTHER
DATE	ID INFORMATION OR CREDIBLE WITNESS	PRINTED NAME & ADDRESS OF SIGNER
TIME ☐ AM ☐ PM		
FEE	☐ PERSONAL KNOWLEDGE	
	☐ DL, PASSPORT OR OTHER ID CARD	
THUMBPRINT	☐ CREDIBLE WITNESS ID & SIGNATURE	
	ADDRESS OF NOTARY OR OTHER INFORMATION	PHONE NO./EMAIL:
		SIGNATURE OF SIGNER
		X

DOCUMENT TYPE/DATE	NOTARIZATION TYPE: ACKNOWLEDGEMENT / JURAT / OTHER	RECORD NO. 166

DATE	ID INFORMATION OR CREDIBLE WITNESS	PRINTED NAME & ADDRESS OF SIGNER
TIME ☐ AM ☐ PM		
FEE	☐ PERSONAL KNOWLEDGE	
	☐ DL, PASSPORT OR OTHER ID CARD	
THUMBPRINT	☐ CREDIBLE WITNESS ID & SIGNATURE	
	ADDRESS OF NOTARY OR OTHER INFORMATION	PHONE NO./EMAIL:
		SIGNATURE OF SIGNER
		X

DOCUMENT TYPE/DATE	NOTARIZATION TYPE: ACKNOWLEDGEMENT / JURAT / OTHER	RECORD NO. 167

DATE	ID INFORMATION OR CREDIBLE WITNESS	PRINTED NAME & ADDRESS OF SIGNER
TIME ☐ AM ☐ PM		
FEE	☐ PERSONAL KNOWLEDGE	
	☐ DL, PASSPORT OR OTHER ID CARD	
THUMBPRINT	☐ CREDIBLE WITNESS ID & SIGNATURE	
	ADDRESS OF NOTARY OR OTHER INFORMATION	PHONE NO./EMAIL:
		SIGNATURE OF SIGNER
		X

DOCUMENT TYPE/DATE	NOTARIZATION TYPE: ACKNOWLEDGEMENT / JURAT / OTHER	RECORD NO. 168

DATE	ID INFORMATION OR CREDIBLE WITNESS	PRINTED NAME & ADDRESS OF SIGNER
TIME ☐ AM ☐ PM		
FEE	☐ PERSONAL KNOWLEDGE	
	☐ DL, PASSPORT OR OTHER ID CARD	
THUMBPRINT	☐ CREDIBLE WITNESS ID & SIGNATURE	
	ADDRESS OF NOTARY OR OTHER INFORMATION	PHONE NO./EMAIL:
		SIGNATURE OF SIGNER
		X

RECORD NO. 169	DOCUMENT TYPE/DATE	NOTARIZATION TYPE: ACKNOWLEDGEMENT / JURAT / OTHER
DATE	ID INFORMATION OR CREDIBLE WITNESS	PRINTED NAME & ADDRESS OF SIGNER
TIME ☐ AM ☐ PM		
FEE	☐ PERSONAL KNOWLEDGE ☐ DL, PASSPORT OR OTHER ID CARD ☐ CREDIBLE WITNESS ID & SIGNATURE	
THUMBPRINT	ADDRESS OF NOTARY OR OTHER INFORMATION	PHONE NO./EMAIL:
		SIGNATURE OF SIGNER
		X

RECORD NO. 170	DOCUMENT TYPE/DATE	NOTARIZATION TYPE: ACKNOWLEDGEMENT / JURAT / OTHER
DATE	ID INFORMATION OR CREDIBLE WITNESS	PRINTED NAME & ADDRESS OF SIGNER
TIME ☐ AM ☐ PM		
FEE	☐ PERSONAL KNOWLEDGE ☐ DL, PASSPORT OR OTHER ID CARD ☐ CREDIBLE WITNESS ID & SIGNATURE	
THUMBPRINT	ADDRESS OF NOTARY OR OTHER INFORMATION	PHONE NO./EMAIL:
		SIGNATURE OF SIGNER
		X

RECORD NO. 171	DOCUMENT TYPE/DATE	NOTARIZATION TYPE: ACKNOWLEDGEMENT / JURAT / OTHER
DATE	ID INFORMATION OR CREDIBLE WITNESS	PRINTED NAME & ADDRESS OF SIGNER
TIME ☐ AM ☐ PM		
FEE	☐ PERSONAL KNOWLEDGE ☐ DL, PASSPORT OR OTHER ID CARD ☐ CREDIBLE WITNESS ID & SIGNATURE	
THUMBPRINT	ADDRESS OF NOTARY OR OTHER INFORMATION	PHONE NO./EMAIL:
		SIGNATURE OF SIGNER
		X

DOCUMENT TYPE/DATE	NOTARIZATION TYPE: ACKNOWLEDGEMENT / JURAT / OTHER	RECORD NO. 172

DATE	ID INFORMATION OR CREDIBLE WITNESS	PRINTED NAME & ADDRESS OF SIGNER
TIME ☐ AM ☐ PM		
FEE	☐ PERSONAL KNOWLEDGE	
THUMBPRINT	☐ DL, PASSPORT OR OTHER ID CARD ☐ CREDIBLE WITNESS ID & SIGNATURE	
	ADDRESS OF NOTARY OR OTHER INFORMATION	PHONE NO./EMAIL:
		SIGNATURE OF SIGNER X

DOCUMENT TYPE/DATE	NOTARIZATION TYPE: ACKNOWLEDGEMENT / JURAT / OTHER	RECORD NO. 173

DATE	ID INFORMATION OR CREDIBLE WITNESS	PRINTED NAME & ADDRESS OF SIGNER
TIME ☐ AM ☐ PM		
FEE	☐ PERSONAL KNOWLEDGE	
THUMBPRINT	☐ DL, PASSPORT OR OTHER ID CARD ☐ CREDIBLE WITNESS ID & SIGNATURE	
	ADDRESS OF NOTARY OR OTHER INFORMATION	PHONE NO./EMAIL:
		SIGNATURE OF SIGNER X

DOCUMENT TYPE/DATE	NOTARIZATION TYPE: ACKNOWLEDGEMENT / JURAT / OTHER	RECORD NO. 174

DATE	ID INFORMATION OR CREDIBLE WITNESS	PRINTED NAME & ADDRESS OF SIGNER
TIME ☐ AM ☐ PM		
FEE	☐ PERSONAL KNOWLEDGE	
THUMBPRINT	☐ DL, PASSPORT OR OTHER ID CARD ☐ CREDIBLE WITNESS ID & SIGNATURE	
	ADDRESS OF NOTARY OR OTHER INFORMATION	PHONE NO./EMAIL:
		SIGNATURE OF SIGNER X

RECORD NO. 175	DOCUMENT TYPE/DATE	NOTARIZATION TYPE: ACKNOWLEDGEMENT / JURAT / OTHER
DATE	ID INFORMATION OR CREDIBLE WITNESS	PRINTED NAME & ADDRESS OF SIGNER
TIME ☐ AM ☐ PM		
FEE	☐ PERSONAL KNOWLEDGE	
	☐ DL, PASSPORT OR OTHER ID CARD	
THUMBPRINT	☐ CREDIBLE WITNESS ID & SIGNATURE	
	ADDRESS OF NOTARY OR OTHER INFORMATION	PHONE NO./EMAIL:
		SIGNATURE OF SIGNER
		X

RECORD NO. 176	DOCUMENT TYPE/DATE	NOTARIZATION TYPE: ACKNOWLEDGEMENT / JURAT / OTHER
DATE	ID INFORMATION OR CREDIBLE WITNESS	PRINTED NAME & ADDRESS OF SIGNER
TIME ☐ AM ☐ PM		
FEE	☐ PERSONAL KNOWLEDGE	
	☐ DL, PASSPORT OR OTHER ID CARD	
THUMBPRINT	☐ CREDIBLE WITNESS ID & SIGNATURE	
	ADDRESS OF NOTARY OR OTHER INFORMATION	PHONE NO./EMAIL:
		SIGNATURE OF SIGNER
		X

RECORD NO. 177	DOCUMENT TYPE/DATE	NOTARIZATION TYPE: ACKNOWLEDGEMENT / JURAT / OTHER
DATE	ID INFORMATION OR CREDIBLE WITNESS	PRINTED NAME & ADDRESS OF SIGNER
TIME ☐ AM ☐ PM		
FEE	☐ PERSONAL KNOWLEDGE	
	☐ DL, PASSPORT OR OTHER ID CARD	
THUMBPRINT	☐ CREDIBLE WITNESS ID & SIGNATURE	
	ADDRESS OF NOTARY OR OTHER INFORMATION	PHONE NO./EMAIL:
		SIGNATURE OF SIGNER
		X

DOCUMENT TYPE/DATE	NOTARIZATION TYPE: ACKNOWLEDGEMENT / JURAT / OTHER	RECORD NO. 178

DATE	ID INFORMATION OR CREDIBLE WITNESS	PRINTED NAME & ADDRESS OF SIGNER
TIME ☐ AM ☐ PM		
FEE	☐ PERSONAL KNOWLEDGE	
THUMBPRINT	☐ DL, PASSPORT OR OTHER ID CARD ☐ CREDIBLE WITNESS ID & SIGNATURE	
	ADDRESS OF NOTARY OR OTHER INFORMATION	PHONE NO./EMAIL:
		SIGNATURE OF SIGNER
		X

DOCUMENT TYPE/DATE	NOTARIZATION TYPE: ACKNOWLEDGEMENT / JURAT / OTHER	RECORD NO. 179

DATE	ID INFORMATION OR CREDIBLE WITNESS	PRINTED NAME & ADDRESS OF SIGNER
TIME ☐ AM ☐ PM		
FEE	☐ PERSONAL KNOWLEDGE	
THUMBPRINT	☐ DL, PASSPORT OR OTHER ID CARD ☐ CREDIBLE WITNESS ID & SIGNATURE	
	ADDRESS OF NOTARY OR OTHER INFORMATION	PHONE NO./EMAIL:
		SIGNATURE OF SIGNER
		X

DOCUMENT TYPE/DATE	NOTARIZATION TYPE: ACKNOWLEDGEMENT / JURAT / OTHER	RECORD NO. 180

DATE	ID INFORMATION OR CREDIBLE WITNESS	PRINTED NAME & ADDRESS OF SIGNER
TIME ☐ AM ☐ PM		
FEE	☐ PERSONAL KNOWLEDGE	
THUMBPRINT	☐ DL, PASSPORT OR OTHER ID CARD ☐ CREDIBLE WITNESS ID & SIGNATURE	
	ADDRESS OF NOTARY OR OTHER INFORMATION	PHONE NO./EMAIL:
		SIGNATURE OF SIGNER
		X

RECORD NO. 181	DOCUMENT TYPE/DATE	NOTARIZATION TYPE: ACKNOWLEDGEMENT / JURAT / OTHER
DATE	ID INFORMATION OR CREDIBLE WITNESS	PRINTED NAME & ADDRESS OF SIGNER
TIME ☐ AM ☐ PM		
FEE	☐ PERSONAL KNOWLEDGE	
	☐ DL, PASSPORT OR OTHER ID CARD	
THUMBPRINT	☐ CREDIBLE WITNESS ID & SIGNATURE	
	ADDRESS OF NOTARY OR OTHER INFORMATION	PHONE NO./EMAIL:
		SIGNATURE OF SIGNER
		X

RECORD NO. 182	DOCUMENT TYPE/DATE	NOTARIZATION TYPE: ACKNOWLEDGEMENT / JURAT / OTHER
DATE	ID INFORMATION OR CREDIBLE WITNESS	PRINTED NAME & ADDRESS OF SIGNER
TIME ☐ AM ☐ PM		
FEE	☐ PERSONAL KNOWLEDGE	
	☐ DL, PASSPORT OR OTHER ID CARD	
THUMBPRINT	☐ CREDIBLE WITNESS ID & SIGNATURE	
	ADDRESS OF NOTARY OR OTHER INFORMATION	PHONE NO./EMAIL:
		SIGNATURE OF SIGNER
		X

RECORD NO. 183	DOCUMENT TYPE/DATE	NOTARIZATION TYPE: ACKNOWLEDGEMENT / JURAT / OTHER
DATE	ID INFORMATION OR CREDIBLE WITNESS	PRINTED NAME & ADDRESS OF SIGNER
TIME ☐ AM ☐ PM		
FEE	☐ PERSONAL KNOWLEDGE	
	☐ DL, PASSPORT OR OTHER ID CARD	
THUMBPRINT	☐ CREDIBLE WITNESS ID & SIGNATURE	
	ADDRESS OF NOTARY OR OTHER INFORMATION	PHONE NO./EMAIL:
		SIGNATURE OF SIGNER
		X

DOCUMENT TYPE/DATE	NOTARIZATION TYPE: ACKNOWLEDGEMENT / JURAT / OTHER	RECORD NO. 184

DATE	ID INFORMATION OR CREDIBLE WITNESS	PRINTED NAME & ADDRESS OF SIGNER
TIME ☐ AM ☐ PM		
FEE	☐ PERSONAL KNOWLEDGE	
THUMBPRINT	☐ DL, PASSPORT OR OTHER ID CARD ☐ CREDIBLE WITNESS ID & SIGNATURE	
	ADDRESS OF NOTARY OR OTHER INFORMATION	PHONE NO./EMAIL:
		SIGNATURE OF SIGNER X

DOCUMENT TYPE/DATE	NOTARIZATION TYPE: ACKNOWLEDGEMENT / JURAT / OTHER	RECORD NO. 185

DATE	ID INFORMATION OR CREDIBLE WITNESS	PRINTED NAME & ADDRESS OF SIGNER
TIME ☐ AM ☐ PM		
FEE	☐ PERSONAL KNOWLEDGE	
THUMBPRINT	☐ DL, PASSPORT OR OTHER ID CARD ☐ CREDIBLE WITNESS ID & SIGNATURE	
	ADDRESS OF NOTARY OR OTHER INFORMATION	PHONE NO./EMAIL:
		SIGNATURE OF SIGNER X

DOCUMENT TYPE/DATE	NOTARIZATION TYPE: ACKNOWLEDGEMENT / JURAT / OTHER	RECORD NO. 186

DATE	ID INFORMATION OR CREDIBLE WITNESS	PRINTED NAME & ADDRESS OF SIGNER
TIME ☐ AM ☐ PM		
FEE	☐ PERSONAL KNOWLEDGE	
THUMBPRINT	☐ DL, PASSPORT OR OTHER ID CARD ☐ CREDIBLE WITNESS ID & SIGNATURE	
	ADDRESS OF NOTARY OR OTHER INFORMATION	PHONE NO./EMAIL:
		SIGNATURE OF SIGNER X

RECORD NO. 187	DOCUMENT TYPE/DATE	NOTARIZATION TYPE: ACKNOWLEDGEMENT / JURAT / OTHER
DATE	ID INFORMATION OR CREDIBLE WITNESS	PRINTED NAME & ADDRESS OF SIGNER
TIME ☐ AM ☐ PM		
FEE	☐ PERSONAL KNOWLEDGE ☐ DL, PASSPORT OR OTHER ID CARD ☐ CREDIBLE WITNESS ID & SIGNATURE	
THUMBPRINT	ADDRESS OF NOTARY OR OTHER INFORMATION	PHONE NO./EMAIL:
		SIGNATURE OF SIGNER X

RECORD NO. 188	DOCUMENT TYPE/DATE	NOTARIZATION TYPE: ACKNOWLEDGEMENT / JURAT / OTHER
DATE	ID INFORMATION OR CREDIBLE WITNESS	PRINTED NAME & ADDRESS OF SIGNER
TIME ☐ AM ☐ PM		
FEE	☐ PERSONAL KNOWLEDGE ☐ DL, PASSPORT OR OTHER ID CARD ☐ CREDIBLE WITNESS ID & SIGNATURE	
THUMBPRINT	ADDRESS OF NOTARY OR OTHER INFORMATION	PHONE NO./EMAIL:
		SIGNATURE OF SIGNER X

RECORD NO. 189	DOCUMENT TYPE/DATE	NOTARIZATION TYPE: ACKNOWLEDGEMENT / JURAT / OTHER
DATE	ID INFORMATION OR CREDIBLE WITNESS	PRINTED NAME & ADDRESS OF SIGNER
TIME ☐ AM ☐ PM		
FEE	☐ PERSONAL KNOWLEDGE ☐ DL, PASSPORT OR OTHER ID CARD ☐ CREDIBLE WITNESS ID & SIGNATURE	
THUMBPRINT	ADDRESS OF NOTARY OR OTHER INFORMATION	PHONE NO./EMAIL:
		SIGNATURE OF SIGNER X

DOCUMENT TYPE/DATE	NOTARIZATION TYPE: ACKNOWLEDGEMENT / JURAT / OTHER	RECORD NO. 190

DATE	ID INFORMATION OR CREDIBLE WITNESS	PRINTED NAME & ADDRESS OF SIGNER
TIME ☐ AM ☐ PM		
FEE	☐ PERSONAL KNOWLEDGE	
	☐ DL, PASSPORT OR OTHER ID CARD	
THUMBPRINT	☐ CREDIBLE WITNESS ID & SIGNATURE	
	ADDRESS OF NOTARY OR OTHER INFORMATION	PHONE NO./EMAIL:
		SIGNATURE OF SIGNER
		X

DOCUMENT TYPE/DATE	NOTARIZATION TYPE: ACKNOWLEDGEMENT / JURAT / OTHER	RECORD NO. 191

DATE	ID INFORMATION OR CREDIBLE WITNESS	PRINTED NAME & ADDRESS OF SIGNER
TIME ☐ AM ☐ PM		
FEE	☐ PERSONAL KNOWLEDGE	
	☐ DL, PASSPORT OR OTHER ID CARD	
THUMBPRINT	☐ CREDIBLE WITNESS ID & SIGNATURE	
	ADDRESS OF NOTARY OR OTHER INFORMATION	PHONE NO./EMAIL:
		SIGNATURE OF SIGNER
		X

DOCUMENT TYPE/DATE	NOTARIZATION TYPE: ACKNOWLEDGEMENT / JURAT / OTHER	RECORD NO. 192

DATE	ID INFORMATION OR CREDIBLE WITNESS	PRINTED NAME & ADDRESS OF SIGNER
TIME ☐ AM ☐ PM		
FEE	☐ PERSONAL KNOWLEDGE	
	☐ DL, PASSPORT OR OTHER ID CARD	
THUMBPRINT	☐ CREDIBLE WITNESS ID & SIGNATURE	
	ADDRESS OF NOTARY OR OTHER INFORMATION	PHONE NO./EMAIL:
		SIGNATURE OF SIGNER
		X

RECORD NO. 193	DOCUMENT TYPE/DATE	NOTARIZATION TYPE: ACKNOWLEDGEMENT / JURAT / OTHER
DATE	ID INFORMATION OR CREDIBLE WITNESS	PRINTED NAME & ADDRESS OF SIGNER
TIME ☐ AM ☐ PM		
FEE	☐ PERSONAL KNOWLEDGE ☐ DL, PASSPORT OR OTHER ID CARD ☐ CREDIBLE WITNESS ID & SIGNATURE	
THUMBPRINT		
	ADDRESS OF NOTARY OR OTHER INFORMATION	PHONE NO./EMAIL:
		SIGNATURE OF SIGNER
		X

RECORD NO. 194	DOCUMENT TYPE/DATE	NOTARIZATION TYPE: ACKNOWLEDGEMENT / JURAT / OTHER
DATE	ID INFORMATION OR CREDIBLE WITNESS	PRINTED NAME & ADDRESS OF SIGNER
TIME ☐ AM ☐ PM		
FEE	☐ PERSONAL KNOWLEDGE ☐ DL, PASSPORT OR OTHER ID CARD ☐ CREDIBLE WITNESS ID & SIGNATURE	
THUMBPRINT		
	ADDRESS OF NOTARY OR OTHER INFORMATION	PHONE NO./EMAIL:
		SIGNATURE OF SIGNER
		X

RECORD NO. 195	DOCUMENT TYPE/DATE	NOTARIZATION TYPE: ACKNOWLEDGEMENT / JURAT / OTHER
DATE	ID INFORMATION OR CREDIBLE WITNESS	PRINTED NAME & ADDRESS OF SIGNER
TIME ☐ AM ☐ PM		
FEE	☐ PERSONAL KNOWLEDGE ☐ DL, PASSPORT OR OTHER ID CARD ☐ CREDIBLE WITNESS ID & SIGNATURE	
THUMBPRINT		
	ADDRESS OF NOTARY OR OTHER INFORMATION	PHONE NO./EMAIL:
		SIGNATURE OF SIGNER
		X

DOCUMENT TYPE/DATE	NOTARIZATION TYPE: ACKNOWLEDGEMENT / JURAT / OTHER	RECORD NO. 196

DATE	ID INFORMATION OR CREDIBLE WITNESS	PRINTED NAME & ADDRESS OF SIGNER
TIME ☐ AM ☐ PM		
FEE	☐ PERSONAL KNOWLEDGE	
THUMBPRINT	☐ DL, PASSPORT OR OTHER ID CARD ☐ CREDIBLE WITNESS ID & SIGNATURE	
	ADDRESS OF NOTARY OR OTHER INFORMATION	PHONE NO./EMAIL:
		SIGNATURE OF SIGNER X

DOCUMENT TYPE/DATE	NOTARIZATION TYPE: ACKNOWLEDGEMENT / JURAT / OTHER	RECORD NO. 197

DATE	ID INFORMATION OR CREDIBLE WITNESS	PRINTED NAME & ADDRESS OF SIGNER
TIME ☐ AM ☐ PM		
FEE	☐ PERSONAL KNOWLEDGE	
THUMBPRINT	☐ DL, PASSPORT OR OTHER ID CARD ☐ CREDIBLE WITNESS ID & SIGNATURE	
	ADDRESS OF NOTARY OR OTHER INFORMATION	PHONE NO./EMAIL:
		SIGNATURE OF SIGNER X

DOCUMENT TYPE/DATE	NOTARIZATION TYPE: ACKNOWLEDGEMENT / JURAT / OTHER	RECORD NO. 198

DATE	ID INFORMATION OR CREDIBLE WITNESS	PRINTED NAME & ADDRESS OF SIGNER
TIME ☐ AM ☐ PM		
FEE	☐ PERSONAL KNOWLEDGE	
THUMBPRINT	☐ DL, PASSPORT OR OTHER ID CARD ☐ CREDIBLE WITNESS ID & SIGNATURE	
	ADDRESS OF NOTARY OR OTHER INFORMATION	PHONE NO./EMAIL:
		SIGNATURE OF SIGNER X

RECORD NO. 199	DOCUMENT TYPE/DATE	NOTARIZATION TYPE: ACKNOWLEDGEMENT / JURAT / OTHER
DATE	ID INFORMATION OR CREDIBLE WITNESS	PRINTED NAME & ADDRESS OF SIGNER
TIME ☐ AM ☐ PM		
FEE	☐ PERSONAL KNOWLEDGE	
THUMBPRINT	☐ DL, PASSPORT OR OTHER ID CARD ☐ CREDIBLE WITNESS ID & SIGNATURE	
	ADDRESS OF NOTARY OR OTHER INFORMATION	PHONE NO./EMAIL:
		SIGNATURE OF SIGNER X

RECORD NO. 200	DOCUMENT TYPE/DATE	NOTARIZATION TYPE: ACKNOWLEDGEMENT / JURAT / OTHER
DATE	ID INFORMATION OR CREDIBLE WITNESS	PRINTED NAME & ADDRESS OF SIGNER
TIME ☐ AM ☐ PM		
FEE	☐ PERSONAL KNOWLEDGE	
THUMBPRINT	☐ DL, PASSPORT OR OTHER ID CARD ☐ CREDIBLE WITNESS ID & SIGNATURE	
	ADDRESS OF NOTARY OR OTHER INFORMATION	PHONE NO./EMAIL:
		SIGNATURE OF SIGNER X

RECORD NO. 201	DOCUMENT TYPE/DATE	NOTARIZATION TYPE: ACKNOWLEDGEMENT / JURAT / OTHER
DATE	ID INFORMATION OR CREDIBLE WITNESS	PRINTED NAME & ADDRESS OF SIGNER
TIME ☐ AM ☐ PM		
FEE	☐ PERSONAL KNOWLEDGE	
THUMBPRINT	☐ DL, PASSPORT OR OTHER ID CARD ☐ CREDIBLE WITNESS ID & SIGNATURE	
	ADDRESS OF NOTARY OR OTHER INFORMATION	PHONE NO./EMAIL:
		SIGNATURE OF SIGNER X

DOCUMENT TYPE/DATE	NOTARIZATION TYPE: ACKNOWLEDGEMENT / JURAT / OTHER	RECORD NO. 202

DATE	ID INFORMATION OR CREDIBLE WITNESS	PRINTED NAME & ADDRESS OF SIGNER
TIME ☐ AM ☐ PM		
FEE	☐ PERSONAL KNOWLEDGE	
THUMBPRINT	☐ DL, PASSPORT OR OTHER ID CARD ☐ CREDIBLE WITNESS ID & SIGNATURE	
	ADDRESS OF NOTARY OR OTHER INFORMATION	PHONE NO./EMAIL:
		SIGNATURE OF SIGNER X

DOCUMENT TYPE/DATE	NOTARIZATION TYPE: ACKNOWLEDGEMENT / JURAT / OTHER	RECORD NO. 203

DATE	ID INFORMATION OR CREDIBLE WITNESS	PRINTED NAME & ADDRESS OF SIGNER
TIME ☐ AM ☐ PM		
FEE	☐ PERSONAL KNOWLEDGE	
THUMBPRINT	☐ DL, PASSPORT OR OTHER ID CARD ☐ CREDIBLE WITNESS ID & SIGNATURE	
	ADDRESS OF NOTARY OR OTHER INFORMATION	PHONE NO./EMAIL:
		SIGNATURE OF SIGNER X

DOCUMENT TYPE/DATE	NOTARIZATION TYPE: ACKNOWLEDGEMENT / JURAT / OTHER	RECORD NO. 204

DATE	ID INFORMATION OR CREDIBLE WITNESS	PRINTED NAME & ADDRESS OF SIGNER
TIME ☐ AM ☐ PM		
FEE	☐ PERSONAL KNOWLEDGE	
THUMBPRINT	☐ DL, PASSPORT OR OTHER ID CARD ☐ CREDIBLE WITNESS ID & SIGNATURE	
	ADDRESS OF NOTARY OR OTHER INFORMATION	PHONE NO./EMAIL:
		SIGNATURE OF SIGNER X

RECORD NO. 205	DOCUMENT TYPE/DATE	NOTARIZATION TYPE: ACKNOWLEDGEMENT / JURAT / OTHER
DATE	ID INFORMATION OR CREDIBLE WITNESS	PRINTED NAME & ADDRESS OF SIGNER
TIME ☐ AM ☐ PM		
FEE	☐ PERSONAL KNOWLEDGE	
	☐ DL, PASSPORT OR OTHER ID CARD	
THUMBPRINT	☐ CREDIBLE WITNESS ID & SIGNATURE	
	ADDRESS OF NOTARY OR OTHER INFORMATION	PHONE NO./EMAIL:
		SIGNATURE OF SIGNER
		X

RECORD NO. 206	DOCUMENT TYPE/DATE	NOTARIZATION TYPE: ACKNOWLEDGEMENT / JURAT / OTHER
DATE	ID INFORMATION OR CREDIBLE WITNESS	PRINTED NAME & ADDRESS OF SIGNER
TIME ☐ AM ☐ PM		
FEE	☐ PERSONAL KNOWLEDGE	
	☐ DL, PASSPORT OR OTHER ID CARD	
THUMBPRINT	☐ CREDIBLE WITNESS ID & SIGNATURE	
	ADDRESS OF NOTARY OR OTHER INFORMATION	PHONE NO./EMAIL:
		SIGNATURE OF SIGNER
		X

RECORD NO. 207	DOCUMENT TYPE/DATE	NOTARIZATION TYPE: ACKNOWLEDGEMENT / JURAT / OTHER
DATE	ID INFORMATION OR CREDIBLE WITNESS	PRINTED NAME & ADDRESS OF SIGNER
TIME ☐ AM ☐ PM		
FEE	☐ PERSONAL KNOWLEDGE	
	☐ DL, PASSPORT OR OTHER ID CARD	
THUMBPRINT	☐ CREDIBLE WITNESS ID & SIGNATURE	
	ADDRESS OF NOTARY OR OTHER INFORMATION	PHONE NO./EMAIL:
		SIGNATURE OF SIGNER
		X

DOCUMENT TYPE/DATE	NOTARIZATION TYPE: ACKNOWLEDGEMENT / JURAT / OTHER	RECORD NO. 208

DATE	ID INFORMATION OR CREDIBLE WITNESS	PRINTED NAME & ADDRESS OF SIGNER
TIME ☐ AM ☐ PM		
FEE	☐ PERSONAL KNOWLEDGE	
	☐ DL, PASSPORT OR OTHER ID CARD	
THUMBPRINT	☐ CREDIBLE WITNESS ID & SIGNATURE	
	ADDRESS OF NOTARY OR OTHER INFORMATION	PHONE NO./EMAIL:
		SIGNATURE OF SIGNER
		X

DOCUMENT TYPE/DATE	NOTARIZATION TYPE: ACKNOWLEDGEMENT / JURAT / OTHER	RECORD NO. 209

DATE	ID INFORMATION OR CREDIBLE WITNESS	PRINTED NAME & ADDRESS OF SIGNER
TIME ☐ AM ☐ PM		
FEE	☐ PERSONAL KNOWLEDGE	
	☐ DL, PASSPORT OR OTHER ID CARD	
THUMBPRINT	☐ CREDIBLE WITNESS ID & SIGNATURE	
	ADDRESS OF NOTARY OR OTHER INFORMATION	PHONE NO./EMAIL:
		SIGNATURE OF SIGNER
		X

DOCUMENT TYPE/DATE	NOTARIZATION TYPE: ACKNOWLEDGEMENT / JURAT / OTHER	RECORD NO. 210

DATE	ID INFORMATION OR CREDIBLE WITNESS	PRINTED NAME & ADDRESS OF SIGNER
TIME ☐ AM ☐ PM		
FEE	☐ PERSONAL KNOWLEDGE	
	☐ DL, PASSPORT OR OTHER ID CARD	
THUMBPRINT	☐ CREDIBLE WITNESS ID & SIGNATURE	
	ADDRESS OF NOTARY OR OTHER INFORMATION	PHONE NO./EMAIL:
		SIGNATURE OF SIGNER
		X

RECORD NO. **211**	DOCUMENT TYPE/DATE	NOTARIZATION TYPE: ACKNOWLEDGEMENT / JURAT / OTHER
DATE	ID INFORMATION OR CREDIBLE WITNESS	PRINTED NAME & ADDRESS OF SIGNER
TIME ☐ AM ☐ PM		
FEE	☐ PERSONAL KNOWLEDGE	
THUMBPRINT	☐ DL, PASSPORT OR OTHER ID CARD ☐ CREDIBLE WITNESS ID & SIGNATURE	
	ADDRESS OF NOTARY OR OTHER INFORMATION	PHONE NO./EMAIL:
		SIGNATURE OF SIGNER
		X

RECORD NO. **212**	DOCUMENT TYPE/DATE	NOTARIZATION TYPE: ACKNOWLEDGEMENT / JURAT / OTHER
DATE	ID INFORMATION OR CREDIBLE WITNESS	PRINTED NAME & ADDRESS OF SIGNER
TIME ☐ AM ☐ PM		
FEE	☐ PERSONAL KNOWLEDGE	
THUMBPRINT	☐ DL, PASSPORT OR OTHER ID CARD ☐ CREDIBLE WITNESS ID & SIGNATURE	
	ADDRESS OF NOTARY OR OTHER INFORMATION	PHONE NO./EMAIL:
		SIGNATURE OF SIGNER
		X

RECORD NO. **213**	DOCUMENT TYPE/DATE	NOTARIZATION TYPE: ACKNOWLEDGEMENT / JURAT / OTHER
DATE	ID INFORMATION OR CREDIBLE WITNESS	PRINTED NAME & ADDRESS OF SIGNER
TIME ☐ AM ☐ PM		
FEE	☐ PERSONAL KNOWLEDGE	
THUMBPRINT	☐ DL, PASSPORT OR OTHER ID CARD ☐ CREDIBLE WITNESS ID & SIGNATURE	
	ADDRESS OF NOTARY OR OTHER INFORMATION	PHONE NO./EMAIL:
		SIGNATURE OF SIGNER
		X

DOCUMENT TYPE/DATE	NOTARIZATION TYPE: ACKNOWLEDGEMENT / JURAT / OTHER	RECORD NO. 214

DATE	ID INFORMATION OR CREDIBLE WITNESS	PRINTED NAME & ADDRESS OF SIGNER
TIME ☐ AM ☐ PM		
FEE	☐ PERSONAL KNOWLEDGE	
	☐ DL, PASSPORT OR OTHER ID CARD	
THUMBPRINT	☐ CREDIBLE WITNESS ID & SIGNATURE	
	ADDRESS OF NOTARY OR OTHER INFORMATION	PHONE NO./EMAIL:
		SIGNATURE OF SIGNER
		X

DOCUMENT TYPE/DATE	NOTARIZATION TYPE: ACKNOWLEDGEMENT / JURAT / OTHER	RECORD NO. 215

DATE	ID INFORMATION OR CREDIBLE WITNESS	PRINTED NAME & ADDRESS OF SIGNER
TIME ☐ AM ☐ PM		
FEE	☐ PERSONAL KNOWLEDGE	
	☐ DL, PASSPORT OR OTHER ID CARD	
THUMBPRINT	☐ CREDIBLE WITNESS ID & SIGNATURE	
	ADDRESS OF NOTARY OR OTHER INFORMATION	PHONE NO./EMAIL:
		SIGNATURE OF SIGNER
		X

DOCUMENT TYPE/DATE	NOTARIZATION TYPE: ACKNOWLEDGEMENT / JURAT / OTHER	RECORD NO. 216

DATE	ID INFORMATION OR CREDIBLE WITNESS	PRINTED NAME & ADDRESS OF SIGNER
TIME ☐ AM ☐ PM		
FEE	☐ PERSONAL KNOWLEDGE	
	☐ DL, PASSPORT OR OTHER ID CARD	
THUMBPRINT	☐ CREDIBLE WITNESS ID & SIGNATURE	
	ADDRESS OF NOTARY OR OTHER INFORMATION	PHONE NO./EMAIL:
		SIGNATURE OF SIGNER
		X

RECORD NO. 217	DOCUMENT TYPE/DATE	NOTARIZATION TYPE: ACKNOWLEDGEMENT / JURAT / OTHER
DATE	ID INFORMATION OR CREDIBLE WITNESS	PRINTED NAME & ADDRESS OF SIGNER
TIME ☐ AM ☐ PM		
FEE	☐ PERSONAL KNOWLEDGE ☐ DL, PASSPORT OR OTHER ID CARD ☐ CREDIBLE WITNESS ID & SIGNATURE	
THUMBPRINT	ADDRESS OF NOTARY OR OTHER INFORMATION	PHONE NO./EMAIL:
		SIGNATURE OF SIGNER X

RECORD NO. 218	DOCUMENT TYPE/DATE	NOTARIZATION TYPE: ACKNOWLEDGEMENT / JURAT / OTHER
DATE	ID INFORMATION OR CREDIBLE WITNESS	PRINTED NAME & ADDRESS OF SIGNER
TIME ☐ AM ☐ PM		
FEE	☐ PERSONAL KNOWLEDGE ☐ DL, PASSPORT OR OTHER ID CARD ☐ CREDIBLE WITNESS ID & SIGNATURE	
THUMBPRINT	ADDRESS OF NOTARY OR OTHER INFORMATION	PHONE NO./EMAIL:
		SIGNATURE OF SIGNER X

RECORD NO. 219	DOCUMENT TYPE/DATE	NOTARIZATION TYPE: ACKNOWLEDGEMENT / JURAT / OTHER
DATE	ID INFORMATION OR CREDIBLE WITNESS	PRINTED NAME & ADDRESS OF SIGNER
TIME ☐ AM ☐ PM		
FEE	☐ PERSONAL KNOWLEDGE ☐ DL, PASSPORT OR OTHER ID CARD ☐ CREDIBLE WITNESS ID & SIGNATURE	
THUMBPRINT	ADDRESS OF NOTARY OR OTHER INFORMATION	PHONE NO./EMAIL:
		SIGNATURE OF SIGNER X

DOCUMENT TYPE/DATE	NOTARIZATION TYPE: ACKNOWLEDGEMENT / JURAT / OTHER	RECORD NO. 220

DATE	ID INFORMATION OR CREDIBLE WITNESS	PRINTED NAME & ADDRESS OF SIGNER
TIME ☐ AM ☐ PM		
FEE	☐ PERSONAL KNOWLEDGE	
THUMBPRINT	☐ DL, PASSPORT OR OTHER ID CARD	
	☐ CREDIBLE WITNESS ID & SIGNATURE	
	ADDRESS OF NOTARY OR OTHER INFORMATION	PHONE NO./EMAIL:
		SIGNATURE OF SIGNER
		X

DOCUMENT TYPE/DATE	NOTARIZATION TYPE: ACKNOWLEDGEMENT / JURAT / OTHER	RECORD NO. 221

DATE	ID INFORMATION OR CREDIBLE WITNESS	PRINTED NAME & ADDRESS OF SIGNER
TIME ☐ AM ☐ PM		
FEE	☐ PERSONAL KNOWLEDGE	
THUMBPRINT	☐ DL, PASSPORT OR OTHER ID CARD	
	☐ CREDIBLE WITNESS ID & SIGNATURE	
	ADDRESS OF NOTARY OR OTHER INFORMATION	PHONE NO./EMAIL:
		SIGNATURE OF SIGNER
		X

DOCUMENT TYPE/DATE	NOTARIZATION TYPE: ACKNOWLEDGEMENT / JURAT / OTHER	RECORD NO. 222

DATE	ID INFORMATION OR CREDIBLE WITNESS	PRINTED NAME & ADDRESS OF SIGNER
TIME ☐ AM ☐ PM		
FEE	☐ PERSONAL KNOWLEDGE	
THUMBPRINT	☐ DL, PASSPORT OR OTHER ID CARD	
	☐ CREDIBLE WITNESS ID & SIGNATURE	
	ADDRESS OF NOTARY OR OTHER INFORMATION	PHONE NO./EMAIL:
		SIGNATURE OF SIGNER
		X

RECORD NO. 223	DOCUMENT TYPE/DATE	NOTARIZATION TYPE: ACKNOWLEDGEMENT / JURAT / OTHER
DATE	ID INFORMATION OR CREDIBLE WITNESS	PRINTED NAME & ADDRESS OF SIGNER
TIME ☐ AM ☐ PM		
FEE	☐ PERSONAL KNOWLEDGE ☐ DL, PASSPORT OR OTHER ID CARD ☐ CREDIBLE WITNESS ID & SIGNATURE	
THUMBPRINT		
	ADDRESS OF NOTARY OR OTHER INFORMATION	PHONE NO./EMAIL:
		SIGNATURE OF SIGNER X

RECORD NO. 224	DOCUMENT TYPE/DATE	NOTARIZATION TYPE: ACKNOWLEDGEMENT / JURAT / OTHER
DATE	ID INFORMATION OR CREDIBLE WITNESS	PRINTED NAME & ADDRESS OF SIGNER
TIME ☐ AM ☐ PM		
FEE	☐ PERSONAL KNOWLEDGE ☐ DL, PASSPORT OR OTHER ID CARD ☐ CREDIBLE WITNESS ID & SIGNATURE	
THUMBPRINT		
	ADDRESS OF NOTARY OR OTHER INFORMATION	PHONE NO./EMAIL:
		SIGNATURE OF SIGNER X

RECORD NO. 225	DOCUMENT TYPE/DATE	NOTARIZATION TYPE: ACKNOWLEDGEMENT / JURAT / OTHER
DATE	ID INFORMATION OR CREDIBLE WITNESS	PRINTED NAME & ADDRESS OF SIGNER
TIME ☐ AM ☐ PM		
FEE	☐ PERSONAL KNOWLEDGE ☐ DL, PASSPORT OR OTHER ID CARD ☐ CREDIBLE WITNESS ID & SIGNATURE	
THUMBPRINT		
	ADDRESS OF NOTARY OR OTHER INFORMATION	PHONE NO./EMAIL:
		SIGNATURE OF SIGNER X

DOCUMENT TYPE/DATE	NOTARIZATION TYPE: ACKNOWLEDGEMENT / JURAT / OTHER	RECORD NO. 226

DATE	ID INFORMATION OR CREDIBLE WITNESS	PRINTED NAME & ADDRESS OF SIGNER
TIME ☐ AM ☐ PM		
FEE	☐ PERSONAL KNOWLEDGE	
THUMBPRINT	☐ DL, PASSPORT OR OTHER ID CARD	
	☐ CREDIBLE WITNESS ID & SIGNATURE	
	ADDRESS OF NOTARY OR OTHER INFORMATION	PHONE NO./EMAIL:
		SIGNATURE OF SIGNER
		X

DOCUMENT TYPE/DATE	NOTARIZATION TYPE: ACKNOWLEDGEMENT / JURAT / OTHER	RECORD NO. 227

DATE	ID INFORMATION OR CREDIBLE WITNESS	PRINTED NAME & ADDRESS OF SIGNER
TIME ☐ AM ☐ PM		
FEE	☐ PERSONAL KNOWLEDGE	
THUMBPRINT	☐ DL, PASSPORT OR OTHER ID CARD	
	☐ CREDIBLE WITNESS ID & SIGNATURE	
	ADDRESS OF NOTARY OR OTHER INFORMATION	PHONE NO./EMAIL:
		SIGNATURE OF SIGNER
		X

DOCUMENT TYPE/DATE	NOTARIZATION TYPE: ACKNOWLEDGEMENT / JURAT / OTHER	RECORD NO. 228

DATE	ID INFORMATION OR CREDIBLE WITNESS	PRINTED NAME & ADDRESS OF SIGNER
TIME ☐ AM ☐ PM		
FEE	☐ PERSONAL KNOWLEDGE	
THUMBPRINT	☐ DL, PASSPORT OR OTHER ID CARD	
	☐ CREDIBLE WITNESS ID & SIGNATURE	
	ADDRESS OF NOTARY OR OTHER INFORMATION	PHONE NO./EMAIL:
		SIGNATURE OF SIGNER
		X

RECORD NO. 229	DOCUMENT TYPE/DATE	NOTARIZATION TYPE: ACKNOWLEDGEMENT / JURAT / OTHER
DATE	ID INFORMATION OR CREDIBLE WITNESS	PRINTED NAME & ADDRESS OF SIGNER
TIME ☐ AM ☐ PM		
FEE	☐ PERSONAL KNOWLEDGE	
	☐ DL, PASSPORT OR OTHER ID CARD	
THUMBPRINT	☐ CREDIBLE WITNESS ID & SIGNATURE	
	ADDRESS OF NOTARY OR OTHER INFORMATION	PHONE NO./EMAIL:
		SIGNATURE OF SIGNER
		X

RECORD NO. 230	DOCUMENT TYPE/DATE	NOTARIZATION TYPE: ACKNOWLEDGEMENT / JURAT / OTHER
DATE	ID INFORMATION OR CREDIBLE WITNESS	PRINTED NAME & ADDRESS OF SIGNER
TIME ☐ AM ☐ PM		
FEE	☐ PERSONAL KNOWLEDGE	
	☐ DL, PASSPORT OR OTHER ID CARD	
THUMBPRINT	☐ CREDIBLE WITNESS ID & SIGNATURE	
	ADDRESS OF NOTARY OR OTHER INFORMATION	PHONE NO./EMAIL:
		SIGNATURE OF SIGNER
		X

RECORD NO. 231	DOCUMENT TYPE/DATE	NOTARIZATION TYPE: ACKNOWLEDGEMENT / JURAT / OTHER
DATE	ID INFORMATION OR CREDIBLE WITNESS	PRINTED NAME & ADDRESS OF SIGNER
TIME ☐ AM ☐ PM		
FEE	☐ PERSONAL KNOWLEDGE	
	☐ DL, PASSPORT OR OTHER ID CARD	
THUMBPRINT	☐ CREDIBLE WITNESS ID & SIGNATURE	
	ADDRESS OF NOTARY OR OTHER INFORMATION	PHONE NO./EMAIL:
		SIGNATURE OF SIGNER
		X

DOCUMENT TYPE/DATE	NOTARIZATION TYPE: ACKNOWLEDGEMENT / JURAT / OTHER	RECORD NO. 232

DATE	ID INFORMATION OR CREDIBLE WITNESS	PRINTED NAME & ADDRESS OF SIGNER
TIME ☐ AM ☐ PM		
FEE	☐ PERSONAL KNOWLEDGE	
THUMBPRINT	☐ DL, PASSPORT OR OTHER ID CARD ☐ CREDIBLE WITNESS ID & SIGNATURE	

ADDRESS OF NOTARY OR OTHER INFORMATION	PHONE NO./EMAIL:
	SIGNATURE OF SIGNER
	X

DOCUMENT TYPE/DATE	NOTARIZATION TYPE: ACKNOWLEDGEMENT / JURAT / OTHER	RECORD NO. 233

DATE	ID INFORMATION OR CREDIBLE WITNESS	PRINTED NAME & ADDRESS OF SIGNER
TIME ☐ AM ☐ PM		
FEE	☐ PERSONAL KNOWLEDGE	
THUMBPRINT	☐ DL, PASSPORT OR OTHER ID CARD ☐ CREDIBLE WITNESS ID & SIGNATURE	

ADDRESS OF NOTARY OR OTHER INFORMATION	PHONE NO./EMAIL:
	SIGNATURE OF SIGNER
	X

DOCUMENT TYPE/DATE	NOTARIZATION TYPE: ACKNOWLEDGEMENT / JURAT / OTHER	RECORD NO. 234

DATE	ID INFORMATION OR CREDIBLE WITNESS	PRINTED NAME & ADDRESS OF SIGNER
TIME ☐ AM ☐ PM		
FEE	☐ PERSONAL KNOWLEDGE	
THUMBPRINT	☐ DL, PASSPORT OR OTHER ID CARD ☐ CREDIBLE WITNESS ID & SIGNATURE	

ADDRESS OF NOTARY OR OTHER INFORMATION	PHONE NO./EMAIL:
	SIGNATURE OF SIGNER
	X

RECORD NO. 235	DOCUMENT TYPE/DATE	NOTARIZATION TYPE: ACKNOWLEDGEMENT / JURAT / OTHER
DATE	ID INFORMATION OR CREDIBLE WITNESS	PRINTED NAME & ADDRESS OF SIGNER
TIME ☐ AM ☐ PM		
FEE	☐ PERSONAL KNOWLEDGE	
	☐ DL, PASSPORT OR OTHER ID CARD	
THUMBPRINT	☐ CREDIBLE WITNESS ID & SIGNATURE	
	ADDRESS OF NOTARY OR OTHER INFORMATION	PHONE NO./EMAIL:
		SIGNATURE OF SIGNER
		X

RECORD NO. 236	DOCUMENT TYPE/DATE	NOTARIZATION TYPE: ACKNOWLEDGEMENT / JURAT / OTHER
DATE	ID INFORMATION OR CREDIBLE WITNESS	PRINTED NAME & ADDRESS OF SIGNER
TIME ☐ AM ☐ PM		
FEE	☐ PERSONAL KNOWLEDGE	
	☐ DL, PASSPORT OR OTHER ID CARD	
THUMBPRINT	☐ CREDIBLE WITNESS ID & SIGNATURE	
	ADDRESS OF NOTARY OR OTHER INFORMATION	PHONE NO./EMAIL:
		SIGNATURE OF SIGNER
		X

RECORD NO. 237	DOCUMENT TYPE/DATE	NOTARIZATION TYPE: ACKNOWLEDGEMENT / JURAT / OTHER
DATE	ID INFORMATION OR CREDIBLE WITNESS	PRINTED NAME & ADDRESS OF SIGNER
TIME ☐ AM ☐ PM		
FEE	☐ PERSONAL KNOWLEDGE	
	☐ DL, PASSPORT OR OTHER ID CARD	
THUMBPRINT	☐ CREDIBLE WITNESS ID & SIGNATURE	
	ADDRESS OF NOTARY OR OTHER INFORMATION	PHONE NO./EMAIL:
		SIGNATURE OF SIGNER
		X

DOCUMENT TYPE/DATE	NOTARIZATION TYPE: ACKNOWLEDGEMENT / JURAT / OTHER	RECORD NO. 238

DATE	ID INFORMATION OR CREDIBLE WITNESS	PRINTED NAME & ADDRESS OF SIGNER
TIME ☐ AM ☐ PM		
FEE	☐ PERSONAL KNOWLEDGE	
	☐ DL, PASSPORT OR OTHER ID CARD	
THUMBPRINT	☐ CREDIBLE WITNESS ID & SIGNATURE	
	ADDRESS OF NOTARY OR OTHER INFORMATION	PHONE NO./EMAIL:
		SIGNATURE OF SIGNER
		X

DOCUMENT TYPE/DATE	NOTARIZATION TYPE: ACKNOWLEDGEMENT / JURAT / OTHER	RECORD NO. 239

DATE	ID INFORMATION OR CREDIBLE WITNESS	PRINTED NAME & ADDRESS OF SIGNER
TIME ☐ AM ☐ PM		
FEE	☐ PERSONAL KNOWLEDGE	
	☐ DL, PASSPORT OR OTHER ID CARD	
THUMBPRINT	☐ CREDIBLE WITNESS ID & SIGNATURE	
	ADDRESS OF NOTARY OR OTHER INFORMATION	PHONE NO./EMAIL:
		SIGNATURE OF SIGNER
		X

DOCUMENT TYPE/DATE	NOTARIZATION TYPE: ACKNOWLEDGEMENT / JURAT / OTHER	RECORD NO. 240

DATE	ID INFORMATION OR CREDIBLE WITNESS	PRINTED NAME & ADDRESS OF SIGNER
TIME ☐ AM ☐ PM		
FEE	☐ PERSONAL KNOWLEDGE	
	☐ DL, PASSPORT OR OTHER ID CARD	
THUMBPRINT	☐ CREDIBLE WITNESS ID & SIGNATURE	
	ADDRESS OF NOTARY OR OTHER INFORMATION	PHONE NO./EMAIL:
		SIGNATURE OF SIGNER
		X

RECORD NO. 241	DOCUMENT TYPE/DATE	NOTARIZATION TYPE: ACKNOWLEDGEMENT / JURAT / OTHER
DATE	ID INFORMATION OR CREDIBLE WITNESS	PRINTED NAME & ADDRESS OF SIGNER
TIME ☐ AM ☐ PM		
FEE	☐ PERSONAL KNOWLEDGE ☐ DL, PASSPORT OR OTHER ID CARD ☐ CREDIBLE WITNESS ID & SIGNATURE	
THUMBPRINT	ADDRESS OF NOTARY OR OTHER INFORMATION	PHONE NO./EMAIL:
		SIGNATURE OF SIGNER X

RECORD NO. 242	DOCUMENT TYPE/DATE	NOTARIZATION TYPE: ACKNOWLEDGEMENT / JURAT / OTHER
DATE	ID INFORMATION OR CREDIBLE WITNESS	PRINTED NAME & ADDRESS OF SIGNER
TIME ☐ AM ☐ PM		
FEE	☐ PERSONAL KNOWLEDGE ☐ DL, PASSPORT OR OTHER ID CARD ☐ CREDIBLE WITNESS ID & SIGNATURE	
THUMBPRINT	ADDRESS OF NOTARY OR OTHER INFORMATION	PHONE NO./EMAIL:
		SIGNATURE OF SIGNER X

RECORD NO. 243	DOCUMENT TYPE/DATE	NOTARIZATION TYPE: ACKNOWLEDGEMENT / JURAT / OTHER
DATE	ID INFORMATION OR CREDIBLE WITNESS	PRINTED NAME & ADDRESS OF SIGNER
TIME ☐ AM ☐ PM		
FEE	☐ PERSONAL KNOWLEDGE ☐ DL, PASSPORT OR OTHER ID CARD ☐ CREDIBLE WITNESS ID & SIGNATURE	
THUMBPRINT	ADDRESS OF NOTARY OR OTHER INFORMATION	PHONE NO./EMAIL:
		SIGNATURE OF SIGNER X

DOCUMENT TYPE/DATE	NOTARIZATION TYPE: ACKNOWLEDGEMENT / JURAT / OTHER	RECORD NO. 244

DATE	ID INFORMATION OR CREDIBLE WITNESS	PRINTED NAME & ADDRESS OF SIGNER
TIME ☐ AM ☐ PM		
FEE	☐ PERSONAL KNOWLEDGE	
	☐ DL, PASSPORT OR OTHER ID CARD	
THUMBPRINT	☐ CREDIBLE WITNESS ID & SIGNATURE	
	ADDRESS OF NOTARY OR OTHER INFORMATION	PHONE NO./EMAIL:
		SIGNATURE OF SIGNER
		X

DOCUMENT TYPE/DATE	NOTARIZATION TYPE: ACKNOWLEDGEMENT / JURAT / OTHER	RECORD NO. 245

DATE	ID INFORMATION OR CREDIBLE WITNESS	PRINTED NAME & ADDRESS OF SIGNER
TIME ☐ AM ☐ PM		
FEE	☐ PERSONAL KNOWLEDGE	
	☐ DL, PASSPORT OR OTHER ID CARD	
THUMBPRINT	☐ CREDIBLE WITNESS ID & SIGNATURE	
	ADDRESS OF NOTARY OR OTHER INFORMATION	PHONE NO./EMAIL:
		SIGNATURE OF SIGNER
		X

DOCUMENT TYPE/DATE	NOTARIZATION TYPE: ACKNOWLEDGEMENT / JURAT / OTHER	RECORD NO. 246

DATE	ID INFORMATION OR CREDIBLE WITNESS	PRINTED NAME & ADDRESS OF SIGNER
TIME ☐ AM ☐ PM		
FEE	☐ PERSONAL KNOWLEDGE	
	☐ DL, PASSPORT OR OTHER ID CARD	
THUMBPRINT	☐ CREDIBLE WITNESS ID & SIGNATURE	
	ADDRESS OF NOTARY OR OTHER INFORMATION	PHONE NO./EMAIL:
		SIGNATURE OF SIGNER
		X

RECORD NO. 247	DOCUMENT TYPE/DATE	NOTARIZATION TYPE: ACKNOWLEDGEMENT / JURAT / OTHER
DATE	ID INFORMATION OR CREDIBLE WITNESS	PRINTED NAME & ADDRESS OF SIGNER
TIME ☐ AM ☐ PM		
FEE	☐ PERSONAL KNOWLEDGE ☐ DL, PASSPORT OR OTHER ID CARD	
THUMBPRINT	☐ CREDIBLE WITNESS ID & SIGNATURE	
	ADDRESS OF NOTARY OR OTHER INFORMATION	PHONE NO./EMAIL:
		SIGNATURE OF SIGNER
		X

RECORD NO. 248	DOCUMENT TYPE/DATE	NOTARIZATION TYPE: ACKNOWLEDGEMENT / JURAT / OTHER
DATE	ID INFORMATION OR CREDIBLE WITNESS	PRINTED NAME & ADDRESS OF SIGNER
TIME ☐ AM ☐ PM		
FEE	☐ PERSONAL KNOWLEDGE ☐ DL, PASSPORT OR OTHER ID CARD	
THUMBPRINT	☐ CREDIBLE WITNESS ID & SIGNATURE	
	ADDRESS OF NOTARY OR OTHER INFORMATION	PHONE NO./EMAIL:
		SIGNATURE OF SIGNER
		X

RECORD NO. 249	DOCUMENT TYPE/DATE	NOTARIZATION TYPE: ACKNOWLEDGEMENT / JURAT / OTHER
DATE	ID INFORMATION OR CREDIBLE WITNESS	PRINTED NAME & ADDRESS OF SIGNER
TIME ☐ AM ☐ PM		
FEE	☐ PERSONAL KNOWLEDGE ☐ DL, PASSPORT OR OTHER ID CARD	
THUMBPRINT	☐ CREDIBLE WITNESS ID & SIGNATURE	
	ADDRESS OF NOTARY OR OTHER INFORMATION	PHONE NO./EMAIL:
		SIGNATURE OF SIGNER
		X

DOCUMENT TYPE/DATE	NOTARIZATION TYPE: ACKNOWLEDGEMENT / JURAT / OTHER	RECORD NO. 250

DATE	ID INFORMATION OR CREDIBLE WITNESS	PRINTED NAME & ADDRESS OF SIGNER
TIME ☐ AM ☐ PM		
FEE	☐ PERSONAL KNOWLEDGE	
	☐ DL, PASSPORT OR OTHER ID CARD	
THUMBPRINT	☐ CREDIBLE WITNESS ID & SIGNATURE	
	ADDRESS OF NOTARY OR OTHER INFORMATION	PHONE NO./EMAIL:
		SIGNATURE OF SIGNER
		X

DOCUMENT TYPE/DATE	NOTARIZATION TYPE: ACKNOWLEDGEMENT / JURAT / OTHER	RECORD NO. 251

DATE	ID INFORMATION OR CREDIBLE WITNESS	PRINTED NAME & ADDRESS OF SIGNER
TIME ☐ AM ☐ PM		
FEE	☐ PERSONAL KNOWLEDGE	
	☐ DL, PASSPORT OR OTHER ID CARD	
THUMBPRINT	☐ CREDIBLE WITNESS ID & SIGNATURE	
	ADDRESS OF NOTARY OR OTHER INFORMATION	PHONE NO./EMAIL:
		SIGNATURE OF SIGNER
		X

DOCUMENT TYPE/DATE	NOTARIZATION TYPE: ACKNOWLEDGEMENT / JURAT / OTHER	RECORD NO. 252

DATE	ID INFORMATION OR CREDIBLE WITNESS	PRINTED NAME & ADDRESS OF SIGNER
TIME ☐ AM ☐ PM		
FEE	☐ PERSONAL KNOWLEDGE	
	☐ DL, PASSPORT OR OTHER ID CARD	
THUMBPRINT	☐ CREDIBLE WITNESS ID & SIGNATURE	
	ADDRESS OF NOTARY OR OTHER INFORMATION	PHONE NO./EMAIL:
		SIGNATURE OF SIGNER
		X

RECORD NO.	DOCUMENT TYPE/DATE	NOTARIZATION TYPE: ACKNOWLEDGEMENT / JURAT / OTHER
253		
DATE	ID INFORMATION OR CREDIBLE WITNESS	PRINTED NAME & ADDRESS OF SIGNER
TIME ☐ AM ☐ PM		
FEE	☐ PERSONAL KNOWLEDGE	
	☐ DL, PASSPORT OR OTHER ID CARD	
THUMBPRINT	☐ CREDIBLE WITNESS ID & SIGNATURE	
	ADDRESS OF NOTARY OR OTHER INFORMATION	PHONE NO./EMAIL:
		SIGNATURE OF SIGNER
		X

RECORD NO.	DOCUMENT TYPE/DATE	NOTARIZATION TYPE: ACKNOWLEDGEMENT / JURAT / OTHER
254		
DATE	ID INFORMATION OR CREDIBLE WITNESS	PRINTED NAME & ADDRESS OF SIGNER
TIME ☐ AM ☐ PM		
FEE	☐ PERSONAL KNOWLEDGE	
	☐ DL, PASSPORT OR OTHER ID CARD	
THUMBPRINT	☐ CREDIBLE WITNESS ID & SIGNATURE	
	ADDRESS OF NOTARY OR OTHER INFORMATION	PHONE NO./EMAIL:
		SIGNATURE OF SIGNER
		X

RECORD NO.	DOCUMENT TYPE/DATE	NOTARIZATION TYPE: ACKNOWLEDGEMENT / JURAT / OTHER
255		
DATE	ID INFORMATION OR CREDIBLE WITNESS	PRINTED NAME & ADDRESS OF SIGNER
TIME ☐ AM ☐ PM		
FEE	☐ PERSONAL KNOWLEDGE	
	☐ DL, PASSPORT OR OTHER ID CARD	
THUMBPRINT	☐ CREDIBLE WITNESS ID & SIGNATURE	
	ADDRESS OF NOTARY OR OTHER INFORMATION	PHONE NO./EMAIL:
		SIGNATURE OF SIGNER
		X

DOCUMENT TYPE/DATE	NOTARIZATION TYPE: ACKNOWLEDGEMENT / JURAT / OTHER	RECORD NO. 256

DATE	ID INFORMATION OR CREDIBLE WITNESS	PRINTED NAME & ADDRESS OF SIGNER
TIME ☐ AM ☐ PM		
FEE	☐ PERSONAL KNOWLEDGE	
	☐ DL, PASSPORT OR OTHER ID CARD	
THUMBPRINT	☐ CREDIBLE WITNESS ID & SIGNATURE	
	ADDRESS OF NOTARY OR OTHER INFORMATION	PHONE NO./EMAIL:
		SIGNATURE OF SIGNER
		X

DOCUMENT TYPE/DATE	NOTARIZATION TYPE: ACKNOWLEDGEMENT / JURAT / OTHER	RECORD NO. 257

DATE	ID INFORMATION OR CREDIBLE WITNESS	PRINTED NAME & ADDRESS OF SIGNER
TIME ☐ AM ☐ PM		
FEE	☐ PERSONAL KNOWLEDGE	
	☐ DL, PASSPORT OR OTHER ID CARD	
THUMBPRINT	☐ CREDIBLE WITNESS ID & SIGNATURE	
	ADDRESS OF NOTARY OR OTHER INFORMATION	PHONE NO./EMAIL:
		SIGNATURE OF SIGNER
		X

DOCUMENT TYPE/DATE	NOTARIZATION TYPE: ACKNOWLEDGEMENT / JURAT / OTHER	RECORD NO. 258

DATE	ID INFORMATION OR CREDIBLE WITNESS	PRINTED NAME & ADDRESS OF SIGNER
TIME ☐ AM ☐ PM		
FEE	☐ PERSONAL KNOWLEDGE	
	☐ DL, PASSPORT OR OTHER ID CARD	
THUMBPRINT	☐ CREDIBLE WITNESS ID & SIGNATURE	
	ADDRESS OF NOTARY OR OTHER INFORMATION	PHONE NO./EMAIL:
		SIGNATURE OF SIGNER
		X

RECORD NO. **259**	DOCUMENT TYPE/DATE	NOTARIZATION TYPE: ACKNOWLEDGEMENT / JURAT / OTHER
DATE	ID INFORMATION OR CREDIBLE WITNESS	PRINTED NAME & ADDRESS OF SIGNER
TIME ☐ AM ☐ PM		
FEE	☐ PERSONAL KNOWLEDGE ☐ DL, PASSPORT OR OTHER ID CARD ☐ CREDIBLE WITNESS ID & SIGNATURE	
THUMBPRINT	ADDRESS OF NOTARY OR OTHER INFORMATION	PHONE NO./EMAIL:
		SIGNATURE OF SIGNER X

RECORD NO. **260**	DOCUMENT TYPE/DATE	NOTARIZATION TYPE: ACKNOWLEDGEMENT / JURAT / OTHER
DATE	ID INFORMATION OR CREDIBLE WITNESS	PRINTED NAME & ADDRESS OF SIGNER
TIME ☐ AM ☐ PM		
FEE	☐ PERSONAL KNOWLEDGE ☐ DL, PASSPORT OR OTHER ID CARD ☐ CREDIBLE WITNESS ID & SIGNATURE	
THUMBPRINT	ADDRESS OF NOTARY OR OTHER INFORMATION	PHONE NO./EMAIL:
		SIGNATURE OF SIGNER X

RECORD NO. **261**	DOCUMENT TYPE/DATE	NOTARIZATION TYPE: ACKNOWLEDGEMENT / JURAT / OTHER
DATE	ID INFORMATION OR CREDIBLE WITNESS	PRINTED NAME & ADDRESS OF SIGNER
TIME ☐ AM ☐ PM		
FEE	☐ PERSONAL KNOWLEDGE ☐ DL, PASSPORT OR OTHER ID CARD ☐ CREDIBLE WITNESS ID & SIGNATURE	
THUMBPRINT	ADDRESS OF NOTARY OR OTHER INFORMATION	PHONE NO./EMAIL:
		SIGNATURE OF SIGNER X

DOCUMENT TYPE/DATE	NOTARIZATION TYPE: ACKNOWLEDGEMENT / JURAT / OTHER	RECORD NO. 262

DATE	ID INFORMATION OR CREDIBLE WITNESS	PRINTED NAME & ADDRESS OF SIGNER
TIME ☐ AM ☐ PM		
FEE	☐ PERSONAL KNOWLEDGE	
	☐ DL, PASSPORT OR OTHER ID CARD	
THUMBPRINT	☐ CREDIBLE WITNESS ID & SIGNATURE	
	ADDRESS OF NOTARY OR OTHER INFORMATION	PHONE NO./EMAIL:
		SIGNATURE OF SIGNER
		X

DOCUMENT TYPE/DATE	NOTARIZATION TYPE: ACKNOWLEDGEMENT / JURAT / OTHER	RECORD NO. 263

DATE	ID INFORMATION OR CREDIBLE WITNESS	PRINTED NAME & ADDRESS OF SIGNER
TIME ☐ AM ☐ PM		
FEE	☐ PERSONAL KNOWLEDGE	
	☐ DL, PASSPORT OR OTHER ID CARD	
THUMBPRINT	☐ CREDIBLE WITNESS ID & SIGNATURE	
	ADDRESS OF NOTARY OR OTHER INFORMATION	PHONE NO./EMAIL:
		SIGNATURE OF SIGNER
		X

DOCUMENT TYPE/DATE	NOTARIZATION TYPE: ACKNOWLEDGEMENT / JURAT / OTHER	RECORD NO. 264

DATE	ID INFORMATION OR CREDIBLE WITNESS	PRINTED NAME & ADDRESS OF SIGNER
TIME ☐ AM ☐ PM		
FEE	☐ PERSONAL KNOWLEDGE	
	☐ DL, PASSPORT OR OTHER ID CARD	
THUMBPRINT	☐ CREDIBLE WITNESS ID & SIGNATURE	
	ADDRESS OF NOTARY OR OTHER INFORMATION	PHONE NO./EMAIL:
		SIGNATURE OF SIGNER
		X

RECORD NO. 265	DOCUMENT TYPE/DATE	NOTARIZATION TYPE: ACKNOWLEDGEMENT / JURAT / OTHER
DATE	ID INFORMATION OR CREDIBLE WITNESS	PRINTED NAME & ADDRESS OF SIGNER
TIME ☐ AM ☐ PM		
FEE	☐ PERSONAL KNOWLEDGE	
	☐ DL, PASSPORT OR OTHER ID CARD	
THUMBPRINT	☐ CREDIBLE WITNESS ID & SIGNATURE	
	ADDRESS OF NOTARY OR OTHER INFORMATION	PHONE NO./EMAIL:
		SIGNATURE OF SIGNER
		X

RECORD NO. 266	DOCUMENT TYPE/DATE	NOTARIZATION TYPE: ACKNOWLEDGEMENT / JURAT / OTHER
DATE	ID INFORMATION OR CREDIBLE WITNESS	PRINTED NAME & ADDRESS OF SIGNER
TIME ☐ AM ☐ PM		
FEE	☐ PERSONAL KNOWLEDGE	
	☐ DL, PASSPORT OR OTHER ID CARD	
THUMBPRINT	☐ CREDIBLE WITNESS ID & SIGNATURE	
	ADDRESS OF NOTARY OR OTHER INFORMATION	PHONE NO./EMAIL:
		SIGNATURE OF SIGNER
		X

RECORD NO. 267	DOCUMENT TYPE/DATE	NOTARIZATION TYPE: ACKNOWLEDGEMENT / JURAT / OTHER
DATE	ID INFORMATION OR CREDIBLE WITNESS	PRINTED NAME & ADDRESS OF SIGNER
TIME ☐ AM ☐ PM		
FEE	☐ PERSONAL KNOWLEDGE	
	☐ DL, PASSPORT OR OTHER ID CARD	
THUMBPRINT	☐ CREDIBLE WITNESS ID & SIGNATURE	
	ADDRESS OF NOTARY OR OTHER INFORMATION	PHONE NO./EMAIL:
		SIGNATURE OF SIGNER
		X

DOCUMENT TYPE/DATE	NOTARIZATION TYPE: ACKNOWLEDGEMENT / JURAT / OTHER	RECORD NO. 268

DATE	ID INFORMATION OR CREDIBLE WITNESS	PRINTED NAME & ADDRESS OF SIGNER
TIME ☐ AM ☐ PM		
FEE	☐ PERSONAL KNOWLEDGE	
	☐ DL, PASSPORT OR OTHER ID CARD	
THUMBPRINT	☐ CREDIBLE WITNESS ID & SIGNATURE	
	ADDRESS OF NOTARY OR OTHER INFORMATION	PHONE NO./EMAIL:
		SIGNATURE OF SIGNER
		X

DOCUMENT TYPE/DATE	NOTARIZATION TYPE: ACKNOWLEDGEMENT / JURAT / OTHER	RECORD NO. 269

DATE	ID INFORMATION OR CREDIBLE WITNESS	PRINTED NAME & ADDRESS OF SIGNER
TIME ☐ AM ☐ PM		
FEE	☐ PERSONAL KNOWLEDGE	
	☐ DL, PASSPORT OR OTHER ID CARD	
THUMBPRINT	☐ CREDIBLE WITNESS ID & SIGNATURE	
	ADDRESS OF NOTARY OR OTHER INFORMATION	PHONE NO./EMAIL:
		SIGNATURE OF SIGNER
		X

DOCUMENT TYPE/DATE	NOTARIZATION TYPE: ACKNOWLEDGEMENT / JURAT / OTHER	RECORD NO. 270

DATE	ID INFORMATION OR CREDIBLE WITNESS	PRINTED NAME & ADDRESS OF SIGNER
TIME ☐ AM ☐ PM		
FEE	☐ PERSONAL KNOWLEDGE	
	☐ DL, PASSPORT OR OTHER ID CARD	
THUMBPRINT	☐ CREDIBLE WITNESS ID & SIGNATURE	
	ADDRESS OF NOTARY OR OTHER INFORMATION	PHONE NO./EMAIL:
		SIGNATURE OF SIGNER
		X

RECORD NO. 271	DOCUMENT TYPE/DATE	NOTARIZATION TYPE: ACKNOWLEDGEMENT / JURAT / OTHER
DATE	ID INFORMATION OR CREDIBLE WITNESS	PRINTED NAME & ADDRESS OF SIGNER
TIME ☐ AM ☐ PM		
FEE	☐ PERSONAL KNOWLEDGE	
	☐ DL, PASSPORT OR OTHER ID CARD	
THUMBPRINT	☐ CREDIBLE WITNESS ID & SIGNATURE	
	ADDRESS OF NOTARY OR OTHER INFORMATION	PHONE NO./EMAIL:
		SIGNATURE OF SIGNER
		X

RECORD NO. 272	DOCUMENT TYPE/DATE	NOTARIZATION TYPE: ACKNOWLEDGEMENT / JURAT / OTHER
DATE	ID INFORMATION OR CREDIBLE WITNESS	PRINTED NAME & ADDRESS OF SIGNER
TIME ☐ AM ☐ PM		
FEE	☐ PERSONAL KNOWLEDGE	
	☐ DL, PASSPORT OR OTHER ID CARD	
THUMBPRINT	☐ CREDIBLE WITNESS ID & SIGNATURE	
	ADDRESS OF NOTARY OR OTHER INFORMATION	PHONE NO./EMAIL:
		SIGNATURE OF SIGNER
		X

RECORD NO. 273	DOCUMENT TYPE/DATE	NOTARIZATION TYPE: ACKNOWLEDGEMENT / JURAT / OTHER
DATE	ID INFORMATION OR CREDIBLE WITNESS	PRINTED NAME & ADDRESS OF SIGNER
TIME ☐ AM ☐ PM		
FEE	☐ PERSONAL KNOWLEDGE	
	☐ DL, PASSPORT OR OTHER ID CARD	
THUMBPRINT	☐ CREDIBLE WITNESS ID & SIGNATURE	
	ADDRESS OF NOTARY OR OTHER INFORMATION	PHONE NO./EMAIL:
		SIGNATURE OF SIGNER
		X

DOCUMENT TYPE/DATE	NOTARIZATION TYPE: ACKNOWLEDGEMENT / JURAT / OTHER	RECORD NO. 274

DATE	ID INFORMATION OR CREDIBLE WITNESS	PRINTED NAME & ADDRESS OF SIGNER
TIME ☐ AM ☐ PM		
FEE	☐ PERSONAL KNOWLEDGE	
	☐ DL, PASSPORT OR OTHER ID CARD	
THUMBPRINT	☐ CREDIBLE WITNESS ID & SIGNATURE	
	ADDRESS OF NOTARY OR OTHER INFORMATION	PHONE NO./EMAIL:
		SIGNATURE OF SIGNER
		X

DOCUMENT TYPE/DATE	NOTARIZATION TYPE: ACKNOWLEDGEMENT / JURAT / OTHER	RECORD NO. 275

DATE	ID INFORMATION OR CREDIBLE WITNESS	PRINTED NAME & ADDRESS OF SIGNER
TIME ☐ AM ☐ PM		
FEE	☐ PERSONAL KNOWLEDGE	
	☐ DL, PASSPORT OR OTHER ID CARD	
THUMBPRINT	☐ CREDIBLE WITNESS ID & SIGNATURE	
	ADDRESS OF NOTARY OR OTHER INFORMATION	PHONE NO./EMAIL:
		SIGNATURE OF SIGNER
		X

DOCUMENT TYPE/DATE	NOTARIZATION TYPE: ACKNOWLEDGEMENT / JURAT / OTHER	RECORD NO. 276

DATE	ID INFORMATION OR CREDIBLE WITNESS	PRINTED NAME & ADDRESS OF SIGNER
TIME ☐ AM ☐ PM		
FEE	☐ PERSONAL KNOWLEDGE	
	☐ DL, PASSPORT OR OTHER ID CARD	
THUMBPRINT	☐ CREDIBLE WITNESS ID & SIGNATURE	
	ADDRESS OF NOTARY OR OTHER INFORMATION	PHONE NO./EMAIL:
		SIGNATURE OF SIGNER
		X

RECORD NO. 277	DOCUMENT TYPE/DATE	NOTARIZATION TYPE: ACKNOWLEDGEMENT / JURAT / OTHER
DATE	ID INFORMATION OR CREDIBLE WITNESS	PRINTED NAME & ADDRESS OF SIGNER
TIME ☐ AM ☐ PM		
FEE	☐ PERSONAL KNOWLEDGE	
THUMBPRINT	☐ DL, PASSPORT OR OTHER ID CARD ☐ CREDIBLE WITNESS ID & SIGNATURE	
	ADDRESS OF NOTARY OR OTHER INFORMATION	PHONE NO./EMAIL:
		SIGNATURE OF SIGNER X

RECORD NO. 278	DOCUMENT TYPE/DATE	NOTARIZATION TYPE: ACKNOWLEDGEMENT / JURAT / OTHER
DATE	ID INFORMATION OR CREDIBLE WITNESS	PRINTED NAME & ADDRESS OF SIGNER
TIME ☐ AM ☐ PM		
FEE	☐ PERSONAL KNOWLEDGE	
THUMBPRINT	☐ DL, PASSPORT OR OTHER ID CARD ☐ CREDIBLE WITNESS ID & SIGNATURE	
	ADDRESS OF NOTARY OR OTHER INFORMATION	PHONE NO./EMAIL:
		SIGNATURE OF SIGNER X

RECORD NO. 279	DOCUMENT TYPE/DATE	NOTARIZATION TYPE: ACKNOWLEDGEMENT / JURAT / OTHER
DATE	ID INFORMATION OR CREDIBLE WITNESS	PRINTED NAME & ADDRESS OF SIGNER
TIME ☐ AM ☐ PM		
FEE	☐ PERSONAL KNOWLEDGE	
THUMBPRINT	☐ DL, PASSPORT OR OTHER ID CARD ☐ CREDIBLE WITNESS ID & SIGNATURE	
	ADDRESS OF NOTARY OR OTHER INFORMATION	PHONE NO./EMAIL:
		SIGNATURE OF SIGNER X

DOCUMENT TYPE/DATE	NOTARIZATION TYPE: ACKNOWLEDGEMENT / JURAT / OTHER	RECORD NO. 280

DATE	ID INFORMATION OR CREDIBLE WITNESS	PRINTED NAME & ADDRESS OF SIGNER
TIME ☐ AM ☐ PM		
FEE	☐ PERSONAL KNOWLEDGE	
THUMBPRINT	☐ DL, PASSPORT OR OTHER ID CARD	
	☐ CREDIBLE WITNESS ID & SIGNATURE	
	ADDRESS OF NOTARY OR OTHER INFORMATION	PHONE NO./EMAIL:
		SIGNATURE OF SIGNER
		X

DOCUMENT TYPE/DATE	NOTARIZATION TYPE: ACKNOWLEDGEMENT / JURAT / OTHER	RECORD NO. 281

DATE	ID INFORMATION OR CREDIBLE WITNESS	PRINTED NAME & ADDRESS OF SIGNER
TIME ☐ AM ☐ PM		
FEE	☐ PERSONAL KNOWLEDGE	
THUMBPRINT	☐ DL, PASSPORT OR OTHER ID CARD	
	☐ CREDIBLE WITNESS ID & SIGNATURE	
	ADDRESS OF NOTARY OR OTHER INFORMATION	PHONE NO./EMAIL:
		SIGNATURE OF SIGNER
		X

DOCUMENT TYPE/DATE	NOTARIZATION TYPE: ACKNOWLEDGEMENT / JURAT / OTHER	RECORD NO. 282

DATE	ID INFORMATION OR CREDIBLE WITNESS	PRINTED NAME & ADDRESS OF SIGNER
TIME ☐ AM ☐ PM		
FEE	☐ PERSONAL KNOWLEDGE	
THUMBPRINT	☐ DL, PASSPORT OR OTHER ID CARD	
	☐ CREDIBLE WITNESS ID & SIGNATURE	
	ADDRESS OF NOTARY OR OTHER INFORMATION	PHONE NO./EMAIL:
		SIGNATURE OF SIGNER
		X

RECORD NO. 283	DOCUMENT TYPE/DATE	NOTARIZATION TYPE: ACKNOWLEDGEMENT / JURAT / OTHER
DATE	ID INFORMATION OR CREDIBLE WITNESS	PRINTED NAME & ADDRESS OF SIGNER
TIME ☐ AM ☐ PM		
FEE	☐ PERSONAL KNOWLEDGE ☐ DL, PASSPORT OR OTHER ID CARD	
THUMBPRINT	☐ CREDIBLE WITNESS ID & SIGNATURE	
	ADDRESS OF NOTARY OR OTHER INFORMATION	PHONE NO./EMAIL:
		SIGNATURE OF SIGNER X

RECORD NO. 284	DOCUMENT TYPE/DATE	NOTARIZATION TYPE: ACKNOWLEDGEMENT / JURAT / OTHER
DATE	ID INFORMATION OR CREDIBLE WITNESS	PRINTED NAME & ADDRESS OF SIGNER
TIME ☐ AM ☐ PM		
FEE	☐ PERSONAL KNOWLEDGE ☐ DL, PASSPORT OR OTHER ID CARD	
THUMBPRINT	☐ CREDIBLE WITNESS ID & SIGNATURE	
	ADDRESS OF NOTARY OR OTHER INFORMATION	PHONE NO./EMAIL:
		SIGNATURE OF SIGNER X

RECORD NO. 285	DOCUMENT TYPE/DATE	NOTARIZATION TYPE: ACKNOWLEDGEMENT / JURAT / OTHER
DATE	ID INFORMATION OR CREDIBLE WITNESS	PRINTED NAME & ADDRESS OF SIGNER
TIME ☐ AM ☐ PM		
FEE	☐ PERSONAL KNOWLEDGE ☐ DL, PASSPORT OR OTHER ID CARD	
THUMBPRINT	☐ CREDIBLE WITNESS ID & SIGNATURE	
	ADDRESS OF NOTARY OR OTHER INFORMATION	PHONE NO./EMAIL:
		SIGNATURE OF SIGNER X

DOCUMENT TYPE/DATE	NOTARIZATION TYPE: ACKNOWLEDGEMENT / JURAT / OTHER	RECORD NO. 286

DATE	ID INFORMATION OR CREDIBLE WITNESS	PRINTED NAME & ADDRESS OF SIGNER
TIME ☐ AM ☐ PM		
FEE	☐ PERSONAL KNOWLEDGE	
THUMBPRINT	☐ DL, PASSPORT OR OTHER ID CARD ☐ CREDIBLE WITNESS ID & SIGNATURE	
	ADDRESS OF NOTARY OR OTHER INFORMATION	PHONE NO./EMAIL:
		SIGNATURE OF SIGNER X

DOCUMENT TYPE/DATE	NOTARIZATION TYPE: ACKNOWLEDGEMENT / JURAT / OTHER	RECORD NO. 287

DATE	ID INFORMATION OR CREDIBLE WITNESS	PRINTED NAME & ADDRESS OF SIGNER
TIME ☐ AM ☐ PM		
FEE	☐ PERSONAL KNOWLEDGE	
THUMBPRINT	☐ DL, PASSPORT OR OTHER ID CARD ☐ CREDIBLE WITNESS ID & SIGNATURE	
	ADDRESS OF NOTARY OR OTHER INFORMATION	PHONE NO./EMAIL:
		SIGNATURE OF SIGNER X

DOCUMENT TYPE/DATE	NOTARIZATION TYPE: ACKNOWLEDGEMENT / JURAT / OTHER	RECORD NO. 288

DATE	ID INFORMATION OR CREDIBLE WITNESS	PRINTED NAME & ADDRESS OF SIGNER
TIME ☐ AM ☐ PM		
FEE	☐ PERSONAL KNOWLEDGE	
THUMBPRINT	☐ DL, PASSPORT OR OTHER ID CARD ☐ CREDIBLE WITNESS ID & SIGNATURE	
	ADDRESS OF NOTARY OR OTHER INFORMATION	PHONE NO./EMAIL:
		SIGNATURE OF SIGNER X

RECORD NO. 289	DOCUMENT TYPE/DATE	NOTARIZATION TYPE: ACKNOWLEDGEMENT / JURAT / OTHER
DATE	ID INFORMATION OR CREDIBLE WITNESS	PRINTED NAME & ADDRESS OF SIGNER
TIME ☐ AM ☐ PM		
FEE	☐ PERSONAL KNOWLEDGE ☐ DL, PASSPORT OR OTHER ID CARD ☐ CREDIBLE WITNESS ID & SIGNATURE	
THUMBPRINT		
	ADDRESS OF NOTARY OR OTHER INFORMATION	PHONE NO./EMAIL:
		SIGNATURE OF SIGNER
		X

RECORD NO. 290	DOCUMENT TYPE/DATE	NOTARIZATION TYPE: ACKNOWLEDGEMENT / JURAT / OTHER
DATE	ID INFORMATION OR CREDIBLE WITNESS	PRINTED NAME & ADDRESS OF SIGNER
TIME ☐ AM ☐ PM		
FEE	☐ PERSONAL KNOWLEDGE ☐ DL, PASSPORT OR OTHER ID CARD ☐ CREDIBLE WITNESS ID & SIGNATURE	
THUMBPRINT		
	ADDRESS OF NOTARY OR OTHER INFORMATION	PHONE NO./EMAIL:
		SIGNATURE OF SIGNER
		X

RECORD NO. 291	DOCUMENT TYPE/DATE	NOTARIZATION TYPE: ACKNOWLEDGEMENT / JURAT / OTHER
DATE	ID INFORMATION OR CREDIBLE WITNESS	PRINTED NAME & ADDRESS OF SIGNER
TIME ☐ AM ☐ PM		
FEE	☐ PERSONAL KNOWLEDGE ☐ DL, PASSPORT OR OTHER ID CARD ☐ CREDIBLE WITNESS ID & SIGNATURE	
THUMBPRINT		
	ADDRESS OF NOTARY OR OTHER INFORMATION	PHONE NO./EMAIL:
		SIGNATURE OF SIGNER
		X

DOCUMENT TYPE/DATE	NOTARIZATION TYPE: ACKNOWLEDGEMENT / JURAT / OTHER	RECORD NO. 292

DATE	ID INFORMATION OR CREDIBLE WITNESS	PRINTED NAME & ADDRESS OF SIGNER
TIME ☐ AM ☐ PM		
FEE	☐ PERSONAL KNOWLEDGE	
	☐ DL, PASSPORT OR OTHER ID CARD	
THUMBPRINT	☐ CREDIBLE WITNESS ID & SIGNATURE	
	ADDRESS OF NOTARY OR OTHER INFORMATION	PHONE NO./EMAIL:
		SIGNATURE OF SIGNER
		X

DOCUMENT TYPE/DATE	NOTARIZATION TYPE: ACKNOWLEDGEMENT / JURAT / OTHER	RECORD NO. 293

DATE	ID INFORMATION OR CREDIBLE WITNESS	PRINTED NAME & ADDRESS OF SIGNER
TIME ☐ AM ☐ PM		
FEE	☐ PERSONAL KNOWLEDGE	
	☐ DL, PASSPORT OR OTHER ID CARD	
THUMBPRINT	☐ CREDIBLE WITNESS ID & SIGNATURE	
	ADDRESS OF NOTARY OR OTHER INFORMATION	PHONE NO./EMAIL:
		SIGNATURE OF SIGNER
		X

DOCUMENT TYPE/DATE	NOTARIZATION TYPE: ACKNOWLEDGEMENT / JURAT / OTHER	RECORD NO. 294

DATE	ID INFORMATION OR CREDIBLE WITNESS	PRINTED NAME & ADDRESS OF SIGNER
TIME ☐ AM ☐ PM		
FEE	☐ PERSONAL KNOWLEDGE	
	☐ DL, PASSPORT OR OTHER ID CARD	
THUMBPRINT	☐ CREDIBLE WITNESS ID & SIGNATURE	
	ADDRESS OF NOTARY OR OTHER INFORMATION	PHONE NO./EMAIL:
		SIGNATURE OF SIGNER
		X

RECORD NO. 295	DOCUMENT TYPE/DATE	NOTARIZATION TYPE: ACKNOWLEDGEMENT / JURAT / OTHER
DATE	ID INFORMATION OR CREDIBLE WITNESS	PRINTED NAME & ADDRESS OF SIGNER
TIME ☐ AM ☐ PM		
FEE	☐ PERSONAL KNOWLEDGE	
	☐ DL, PASSPORT OR OTHER ID CARD	
THUMBPRINT	☐ CREDIBLE WITNESS ID & SIGNATURE	
	ADDRESS OF NOTARY OR OTHER INFORMATION	PHONE NO./EMAIL:
		SIGNATURE OF SIGNER
		X

RECORD NO. 296	DOCUMENT TYPE/DATE	NOTARIZATION TYPE: ACKNOWLEDGEMENT / JURAT / OTHER
DATE	ID INFORMATION OR CREDIBLE WITNESS	PRINTED NAME & ADDRESS OF SIGNER
TIME ☐ AM ☐ PM		
FEE	☐ PERSONAL KNOWLEDGE	
	☐ DL, PASSPORT OR OTHER ID CARD	
THUMBPRINT	☐ CREDIBLE WITNESS ID & SIGNATURE	
	ADDRESS OF NOTARY OR OTHER INFORMATION	PHONE NO./EMAIL:
		SIGNATURE OF SIGNER
		X

RECORD NO. 297	DOCUMENT TYPE/DATE	NOTARIZATION TYPE: ACKNOWLEDGEMENT / JURAT / OTHER
DATE	ID INFORMATION OR CREDIBLE WITNESS	PRINTED NAME & ADDRESS OF SIGNER
TIME ☐ AM ☐ PM		
FEE	☐ PERSONAL KNOWLEDGE	
	☐ DL, PASSPORT OR OTHER ID CARD	
THUMBPRINT	☐ CREDIBLE WITNESS ID & SIGNATURE	
	ADDRESS OF NOTARY OR OTHER INFORMATION	PHONE NO./EMAIL:
		SIGNATURE OF SIGNER
		X

DOCUMENT TYPE/DATE	NOTARIZATION TYPE: ACKNOWLEDGEMENT / JURAT / OTHER	RECORD NO. 298

DATE	ID INFORMATION OR CREDIBLE WITNESS	PRINTED NAME & ADDRESS OF SIGNER
TIME ☐ AM ☐ PM		
FEE	☐ PERSONAL KNOWLEDGE	
	☐ DL, PASSPORT OR OTHER ID CARD	
THUMBPRINT	☐ CREDIBLE WITNESS ID & SIGNATURE	

ADDRESS OF NOTARY OR OTHER INFORMATION	PHONE NO./EMAIL:
	SIGNATURE OF SIGNER
	X

DOCUMENT TYPE/DATE	NOTARIZATION TYPE: ACKNOWLEDGEMENT / JURAT / OTHER	RECORD NO. 299

DATE	ID INFORMATION OR CREDIBLE WITNESS	PRINTED NAME & ADDRESS OF SIGNER
TIME ☐ AM ☐ PM		
FEE	☐ PERSONAL KNOWLEDGE	
	☐ DL, PASSPORT OR OTHER ID CARD	
THUMBPRINT	☐ CREDIBLE WITNESS ID & SIGNATURE	

ADDRESS OF NOTARY OR OTHER INFORMATION	PHONE NO./EMAIL:
	SIGNATURE OF SIGNER
	X

DOCUMENT TYPE/DATE	NOTARIZATION TYPE: ACKNOWLEDGEMENT / JURAT / OTHER	RECORD NO. 300

DATE	ID INFORMATION OR CREDIBLE WITNESS	PRINTED NAME & ADDRESS OF SIGNER
TIME ☐ AM ☐ PM		
FEE	☐ PERSONAL KNOWLEDGE	
	☐ DL, PASSPORT OR OTHER ID CARD	
THUMBPRINT	☐ CREDIBLE WITNESS ID & SIGNATURE	

ADDRESS OF NOTARY OR OTHER INFORMATION	PHONE NO./EMAIL:
	SIGNATURE OF SIGNER
	X

RECORD NO. 301	DOCUMENT TYPE/DATE	NOTARIZATION TYPE: ACKNOWLEDGEMENT / JURAT / OTHER
DATE	ID INFORMATION OR CREDIBLE WITNESS	PRINTED NAME & ADDRESS OF SIGNER
TIME ☐ AM ☐ PM		
FEE	☐ PERSONAL KNOWLEDGE	
	☐ DL, PASSPORT OR OTHER ID CARD	
THUMBPRINT	☐ CREDIBLE WITNESS ID & SIGNATURE	
	ADDRESS OF NOTARY OR OTHER INFORMATION	PHONE NO./EMAIL:
		SIGNATURE OF SIGNER
		X

RECORD NO. 302	DOCUMENT TYPE/DATE	NOTARIZATION TYPE: ACKNOWLEDGEMENT / JURAT / OTHER
DATE	ID INFORMATION OR CREDIBLE WITNESS	PRINTED NAME & ADDRESS OF SIGNER
TIME ☐ AM ☐ PM		
FEE	☐ PERSONAL KNOWLEDGE	
	☐ DL, PASSPORT OR OTHER ID CARD	
THUMBPRINT	☐ CREDIBLE WITNESS ID & SIGNATURE	
	ADDRESS OF NOTARY OR OTHER INFORMATION	PHONE NO./EMAIL:
		SIGNATURE OF SIGNER
		X

RECORD NO. 303	DOCUMENT TYPE/DATE	NOTARIZATION TYPE: ACKNOWLEDGEMENT / JURAT / OTHER
DATE	ID INFORMATION OR CREDIBLE WITNESS	PRINTED NAME & ADDRESS OF SIGNER
TIME ☐ AM ☐ PM		
FEE	☐ PERSONAL KNOWLEDGE	
	☐ DL, PASSPORT OR OTHER ID CARD	
THUMBPRINT	☐ CREDIBLE WITNESS ID & SIGNATURE	
	ADDRESS OF NOTARY OR OTHER INFORMATION	PHONE NO./EMAIL:
		SIGNATURE OF SIGNER
		X

DOCUMENT TYPE/DATE	NOTARIZATION TYPE: ACKNOWLEDGEMENT / JURAT / OTHER	RECORD NO. 304

DATE	ID INFORMATION OR CREDIBLE WITNESS	PRINTED NAME & ADDRESS OF SIGNER
TIME ☐ AM ☐ PM		
FEE	☐ PERSONAL KNOWLEDGE	
	☐ DL, PASSPORT OR OTHER ID CARD	
THUMBPRINT	☐ CREDIBLE WITNESS ID & SIGNATURE	
	ADDRESS OF NOTARY OR OTHER INFORMATION	PHONE NO./EMAIL:
		SIGNATURE OF SIGNER
		X

DOCUMENT TYPE/DATE	NOTARIZATION TYPE: ACKNOWLEDGEMENT / JURAT / OTHER	RECORD NO. 305

DATE	ID INFORMATION OR CREDIBLE WITNESS	PRINTED NAME & ADDRESS OF SIGNER
TIME ☐ AM ☐ PM		
FEE	☐ PERSONAL KNOWLEDGE	
	☐ DL, PASSPORT OR OTHER ID CARD	
THUMBPRINT	☐ CREDIBLE WITNESS ID & SIGNATURE	
	ADDRESS OF NOTARY OR OTHER INFORMATION	PHONE NO./EMAIL:
		SIGNATURE OF SIGNER
		X

DOCUMENT TYPE/DATE	NOTARIZATION TYPE: ACKNOWLEDGEMENT / JURAT / OTHER	RECORD NO. 306

DATE	ID INFORMATION OR CREDIBLE WITNESS	PRINTED NAME & ADDRESS OF SIGNER
TIME ☐ AM ☐ PM		
FEE	☐ PERSONAL KNOWLEDGE	
	☐ DL, PASSPORT OR OTHER ID CARD	
THUMBPRINT	☐ CREDIBLE WITNESS ID & SIGNATURE	
	ADDRESS OF NOTARY OR OTHER INFORMATION	PHONE NO./EMAIL:
		SIGNATURE OF SIGNER
		X

RECORD NO. 307	DOCUMENT TYPE/DATE	NOTARIZATION TYPE: ACKNOWLEDGEMENT / JURAT / OTHER
DATE	ID INFORMATION OR CREDIBLE WITNESS	PRINTED NAME & ADDRESS OF SIGNER
TIME ☐ AM ☐ PM		
FEE	☐ PERSONAL KNOWLEDGE	
	☐ DL, PASSPORT OR OTHER ID CARD	
THUMBPRINT	☐ CREDIBLE WITNESS ID & SIGNATURE	
	ADDRESS OF NOTARY OR OTHER INFORMATION	PHONE NO./EMAIL:
		SIGNATURE OF SIGNER
		X

RECORD NO. 308	DOCUMENT TYPE/DATE	NOTARIZATION TYPE: ACKNOWLEDGEMENT / JURAT / OTHER
DATE	ID INFORMATION OR CREDIBLE WITNESS	PRINTED NAME & ADDRESS OF SIGNER
TIME ☐ AM ☐ PM		
FEE	☐ PERSONAL KNOWLEDGE	
	☐ DL, PASSPORT OR OTHER ID CARD	
THUMBPRINT	☐ CREDIBLE WITNESS ID & SIGNATURE	
	ADDRESS OF NOTARY OR OTHER INFORMATION	PHONE NO./EMAIL:
		SIGNATURE OF SIGNER
		X

RECORD NO. 309	DOCUMENT TYPE/DATE	NOTARIZATION TYPE: ACKNOWLEDGEMENT / JURAT / OTHER
DATE	ID INFORMATION OR CREDIBLE WITNESS	PRINTED NAME & ADDRESS OF SIGNER
TIME ☐ AM ☐ PM		
FEE	☐ PERSONAL KNOWLEDGE	
	☐ DL, PASSPORT OR OTHER ID CARD	
THUMBPRINT	☐ CREDIBLE WITNESS ID & SIGNATURE	
	ADDRESS OF NOTARY OR OTHER INFORMATION	PHONE NO./EMAIL:
		SIGNATURE OF SIGNER
		X

DOCUMENT TYPE/DATE	NOTARIZATION TYPE: ACKNOWLEDGEMENT / JURAT / OTHER	RECORD NO. 310

DATE	ID INFORMATION OR CREDIBLE WITNESS	PRINTED NAME & ADDRESS OF SIGNER
TIME ☐ AM ☐ PM		
FEE	☐ PERSONAL KNOWLEDGE	
THUMBPRINT	☐ DL, PASSPORT OR OTHER ID CARD ☐ CREDIBLE WITNESS ID & SIGNATURE	
	ADDRESS OF NOTARY OR OTHER INFORMATION	PHONE NO./EMAIL:
		SIGNATURE OF SIGNER X

DOCUMENT TYPE/DATE	NOTARIZATION TYPE: ACKNOWLEDGEMENT / JURAT / OTHER	RECORD NO. 311

DATE	ID INFORMATION OR CREDIBLE WITNESS	PRINTED NAME & ADDRESS OF SIGNER
TIME ☐ AM ☐ PM		
FEE	☐ PERSONAL KNOWLEDGE	
THUMBPRINT	☐ DL, PASSPORT OR OTHER ID CARD ☐ CREDIBLE WITNESS ID & SIGNATURE	
	ADDRESS OF NOTARY OR OTHER INFORMATION	PHONE NO./EMAIL:
		SIGNATURE OF SIGNER X

DOCUMENT TYPE/DATE	NOTARIZATION TYPE: ACKNOWLEDGEMENT / JURAT / OTHER	RECORD NO. 312

DATE	ID INFORMATION OR CREDIBLE WITNESS	PRINTED NAME & ADDRESS OF SIGNER
TIME ☐ AM ☐ PM		
FEE	☐ PERSONAL KNOWLEDGE	
THUMBPRINT	☐ DL, PASSPORT OR OTHER ID CARD ☐ CREDIBLE WITNESS ID & SIGNATURE	
	ADDRESS OF NOTARY OR OTHER INFORMATION	PHONE NO./EMAIL:
		SIGNATURE OF SIGNER X

RECORD NO. 313	DOCUMENT TYPE/DATE	NOTARIZATION TYPE: ACKNOWLEDGEMENT / JURAT / OTHER
DATE	ID INFORMATION OR CREDIBLE WITNESS	PRINTED NAME & ADDRESS OF SIGNER
TIME ☐ AM ☐ PM		
FEE	☐ PERSONAL KNOWLEDGE ☐ DL, PASSPORT OR OTHER ID CARD ☐ CREDIBLE WITNESS ID & SIGNATURE	
THUMBPRINT		
	ADDRESS OF NOTARY OR OTHER INFORMATION	PHONE NO./EMAIL:
		SIGNATURE OF SIGNER X

RECORD NO. 314	DOCUMENT TYPE/DATE	NOTARIZATION TYPE: ACKNOWLEDGEMENT / JURAT / OTHER
DATE	ID INFORMATION OR CREDIBLE WITNESS	PRINTED NAME & ADDRESS OF SIGNER
TIME ☐ AM ☐ PM		
FEE	☐ PERSONAL KNOWLEDGE ☐ DL, PASSPORT OR OTHER ID CARD ☐ CREDIBLE WITNESS ID & SIGNATURE	
THUMBPRINT		
	ADDRESS OF NOTARY OR OTHER INFORMATION	PHONE NO./EMAIL:
		SIGNATURE OF SIGNER X

RECORD NO. 315	DOCUMENT TYPE/DATE	NOTARIZATION TYPE: ACKNOWLEDGEMENT / JURAT / OTHER
DATE	ID INFORMATION OR CREDIBLE WITNESS	PRINTED NAME & ADDRESS OF SIGNER
TIME ☐ AM ☐ PM		
FEE	☐ PERSONAL KNOWLEDGE ☐ DL, PASSPORT OR OTHER ID CARD ☐ CREDIBLE WITNESS ID & SIGNATURE	
THUMBPRINT		
	ADDRESS OF NOTARY OR OTHER INFORMATION	PHONE NO./EMAIL:
		SIGNATURE OF SIGNER X

DOCUMENT TYPE/DATE	NOTARIZATION TYPE: ACKNOWLEDGEMENT / JURAT / OTHER	RECORD NO. 316

DATE	ID INFORMATION OR CREDIBLE WITNESS	PRINTED NAME & ADDRESS OF SIGNER
TIME ☐ AM ☐ PM		
FEE	☐ PERSONAL KNOWLEDGE	
	☐ DL, PASSPORT OR OTHER ID CARD	
THUMBPRINT	☐ CREDIBLE WITNESS ID & SIGNATURE	
	ADDRESS OF NOTARY OR OTHER INFORMATION	PHONE NO./EMAIL:
		SIGNATURE OF SIGNER
		X

DOCUMENT TYPE/DATE	NOTARIZATION TYPE: ACKNOWLEDGEMENT / JURAT / OTHER	RECORD NO. 317

DATE	ID INFORMATION OR CREDIBLE WITNESS	PRINTED NAME & ADDRESS OF SIGNER
TIME ☐ AM ☐ PM		
FEE	☐ PERSONAL KNOWLEDGE	
	☐ DL, PASSPORT OR OTHER ID CARD	
THUMBPRINT	☐ CREDIBLE WITNESS ID & SIGNATURE	
	ADDRESS OF NOTARY OR OTHER INFORMATION	PHONE NO./EMAIL:
		SIGNATURE OF SIGNER
		X

DOCUMENT TYPE/DATE	NOTARIZATION TYPE: ACKNOWLEDGEMENT / JURAT / OTHER	RECORD NO. 318

DATE	ID INFORMATION OR CREDIBLE WITNESS	PRINTED NAME & ADDRESS OF SIGNER
TIME ☐ AM ☐ PM		
FEE	☐ PERSONAL KNOWLEDGE	
	☐ DL, PASSPORT OR OTHER ID CARD	
THUMBPRINT	☐ CREDIBLE WITNESS ID & SIGNATURE	
	ADDRESS OF NOTARY OR OTHER INFORMATION	PHONE NO./EMAIL:
		SIGNATURE OF SIGNER
		X

RECORD NO. 319	DOCUMENT TYPE/DATE	NOTARIZATION TYPE: ACKNOWLEDGEMENT / JURAT / OTHER
DATE	ID INFORMATION OR CREDIBLE WITNESS	PRINTED NAME & ADDRESS OF SIGNER
TIME ☐ AM ☐ PM		
FEE	☐ PERSONAL KNOWLEDGE ☐ DL, PASSPORT OR OTHER ID CARD ☐ CREDIBLE WITNESS ID & SIGNATURE	
THUMBPRINT		
	ADDRESS OF NOTARY OR OTHER INFORMATION	PHONE NO./EMAIL:
		SIGNATURE OF SIGNER X

RECORD NO. 320	DOCUMENT TYPE/DATE	NOTARIZATION TYPE: ACKNOWLEDGEMENT / JURAT / OTHER
DATE	ID INFORMATION OR CREDIBLE WITNESS	PRINTED NAME & ADDRESS OF SIGNER
TIME ☐ AM ☐ PM		
FEE	☐ PERSONAL KNOWLEDGE ☐ DL, PASSPORT OR OTHER ID CARD ☐ CREDIBLE WITNESS ID & SIGNATURE	
THUMBPRINT		
	ADDRESS OF NOTARY OR OTHER INFORMATION	PHONE NO./EMAIL:
		SIGNATURE OF SIGNER X

RECORD NO. 321	DOCUMENT TYPE/DATE	NOTARIZATION TYPE: ACKNOWLEDGEMENT / JURAT / OTHER
DATE	ID INFORMATION OR CREDIBLE WITNESS	PRINTED NAME & ADDRESS OF SIGNER
TIME ☐ AM ☐ PM		
FEE	☐ PERSONAL KNOWLEDGE ☐ DL, PASSPORT OR OTHER ID CARD ☐ CREDIBLE WITNESS ID & SIGNATURE	
THUMBPRINT		
	ADDRESS OF NOTARY OR OTHER INFORMATION	PHONE NO./EMAIL:
		SIGNATURE OF SIGNER X

DOCUMENT TYPE/DATE	NOTARIZATION TYPE: ACKNOWLEDGEMENT / JURAT / OTHER	RECORD NO. 322

DATE	ID INFORMATION OR CREDIBLE WITNESS	PRINTED NAME & ADDRESS OF SIGNER
TIME ☐ AM ☐ PM		
FEE	☐ PERSONAL KNOWLEDGE	
THUMBPRINT	☐ DL, PASSPORT OR OTHER ID CARD ☐ CREDIBLE WITNESS ID & SIGNATURE	
	ADDRESS OF NOTARY OR OTHER INFORMATION	PHONE NO./EMAIL:
		SIGNATURE OF SIGNER X

DOCUMENT TYPE/DATE	NOTARIZATION TYPE: ACKNOWLEDGEMENT / JURAT / OTHER	RECORD NO. 323

DATE	ID INFORMATION OR CREDIBLE WITNESS	PRINTED NAME & ADDRESS OF SIGNER
TIME ☐ AM ☐ PM		
FEE	☐ PERSONAL KNOWLEDGE	
THUMBPRINT	☐ DL, PASSPORT OR OTHER ID CARD ☐ CREDIBLE WITNESS ID & SIGNATURE	
	ADDRESS OF NOTARY OR OTHER INFORMATION	PHONE NO./EMAIL:
		SIGNATURE OF SIGNER X

DOCUMENT TYPE/DATE	NOTARIZATION TYPE: ACKNOWLEDGEMENT / JURAT / OTHER	RECORD NO. 324

DATE	ID INFORMATION OR CREDIBLE WITNESS	PRINTED NAME & ADDRESS OF SIGNER
TIME ☐ AM ☐ PM		
FEE	☐ PERSONAL KNOWLEDGE	
THUMBPRINT	☐ DL, PASSPORT OR OTHER ID CARD ☐ CREDIBLE WITNESS ID & SIGNATURE	
	ADDRESS OF NOTARY OR OTHER INFORMATION	PHONE NO./EMAIL:
		SIGNATURE OF SIGNER X

RECORD NO. 325	DOCUMENT TYPE/DATE	NOTARIZATION TYPE: ACKNOWLEDGEMENT / JURAT / OTHER
DATE	ID INFORMATION OR CREDIBLE WITNESS	PRINTED NAME & ADDRESS OF SIGNER
TIME ☐ AM ☐ PM		
FEE	☐ PERSONAL KNOWLEDGE	
	☐ DL, PASSPORT OR OTHER ID CARD	
THUMBPRINT	☐ CREDIBLE WITNESS ID & SIGNATURE	
	ADDRESS OF NOTARY OR OTHER INFORMATION	PHONE NO./EMAIL:
		SIGNATURE OF SIGNER
		X

RECORD NO. 326	DOCUMENT TYPE/DATE	NOTARIZATION TYPE: ACKNOWLEDGEMENT / JURAT / OTHER
DATE	ID INFORMATION OR CREDIBLE WITNESS	PRINTED NAME & ADDRESS OF SIGNER
TIME ☐ AM ☐ PM		
FEE	☐ PERSONAL KNOWLEDGE	
	☐ DL, PASSPORT OR OTHER ID CARD	
THUMBPRINT	☐ CREDIBLE WITNESS ID & SIGNATURE	
	ADDRESS OF NOTARY OR OTHER INFORMATION	PHONE NO./EMAIL:
		SIGNATURE OF SIGNER
		X

RECORD NO. 327	DOCUMENT TYPE/DATE	NOTARIZATION TYPE: ACKNOWLEDGEMENT / JURAT / OTHER
DATE	ID INFORMATION OR CREDIBLE WITNESS	PRINTED NAME & ADDRESS OF SIGNER
TIME ☐ AM ☐ PM		
FEE	☐ PERSONAL KNOWLEDGE	
	☐ DL, PASSPORT OR OTHER ID CARD	
THUMBPRINT	☐ CREDIBLE WITNESS ID & SIGNATURE	
	ADDRESS OF NOTARY OR OTHER INFORMATION	PHONE NO./EMAIL:
		SIGNATURE OF SIGNER
		X

DOCUMENT TYPE/DATE	NOTARIZATION TYPE: ACKNOWLEDGEMENT / JURAT / OTHER	RECORD NO. 328

DATE	ID INFORMATION OR CREDIBLE WITNESS	PRINTED NAME & ADDRESS OF SIGNER
TIME ☐ AM ☐ PM		
FEE	☐ PERSONAL KNOWLEDGE	
THUMBPRINT	☐ DL, PASSPORT OR OTHER ID CARD ☐ CREDIBLE WITNESS ID & SIGNATURE	
	ADDRESS OF NOTARY OR OTHER INFORMATION	PHONE NO./EMAIL:
		SIGNATURE OF SIGNER X

DOCUMENT TYPE/DATE	NOTARIZATION TYPE: ACKNOWLEDGEMENT / JURAT / OTHER	RECORD NO. 329

DATE	ID INFORMATION OR CREDIBLE WITNESS	PRINTED NAME & ADDRESS OF SIGNER
TIME ☐ AM ☐ PM		
FEE	☐ PERSONAL KNOWLEDGE	
THUMBPRINT	☐ DL, PASSPORT OR OTHER ID CARD ☐ CREDIBLE WITNESS ID & SIGNATURE	
	ADDRESS OF NOTARY OR OTHER INFORMATION	PHONE NO./EMAIL:
		SIGNATURE OF SIGNER X

DOCUMENT TYPE/DATE	NOTARIZATION TYPE: ACKNOWLEDGEMENT / JURAT / OTHER	RECORD NO. 330

DATE	ID INFORMATION OR CREDIBLE WITNESS	PRINTED NAME & ADDRESS OF SIGNER
TIME ☐ AM ☐ PM		
FEE	☐ PERSONAL KNOWLEDGE	
THUMBPRINT	☐ DL, PASSPORT OR OTHER ID CARD ☐ CREDIBLE WITNESS ID & SIGNATURE	
	ADDRESS OF NOTARY OR OTHER INFORMATION	PHONE NO./EMAIL:
		SIGNATURE OF SIGNER X

RECORD NO. 331	DOCUMENT TYPE/DATE	NOTARIZATION TYPE: ACKNOWLEDGEMENT / JURAT / OTHER
DATE	ID INFORMATION OR CREDIBLE WITNESS	PRINTED NAME & ADDRESS OF SIGNER
TIME ☐ AM ☐ PM		
FEE	☐ PERSONAL KNOWLEDGE	
	☐ DL, PASSPORT OR OTHER ID CARD	
THUMBPRINT	☐ CREDIBLE WITNESS ID & SIGNATURE	
	ADDRESS OF NOTARY OR OTHER INFORMATION	PHONE NO./EMAIL:
		SIGNATURE OF SIGNER
		X

RECORD NO. 332	DOCUMENT TYPE/DATE	NOTARIZATION TYPE: ACKNOWLEDGEMENT / JURAT / OTHER
DATE	ID INFORMATION OR CREDIBLE WITNESS	PRINTED NAME & ADDRESS OF SIGNER
TIME ☐ AM ☐ PM		
FEE	☐ PERSONAL KNOWLEDGE	
	☐ DL, PASSPORT OR OTHER ID CARD	
THUMBPRINT	☐ CREDIBLE WITNESS ID & SIGNATURE	
	ADDRESS OF NOTARY OR OTHER INFORMATION	PHONE NO./EMAIL:
		SIGNATURE OF SIGNER
		X

RECORD NO. 333	DOCUMENT TYPE/DATE	NOTARIZATION TYPE: ACKNOWLEDGEMENT / JURAT / OTHER
DATE	ID INFORMATION OR CREDIBLE WITNESS	PRINTED NAME & ADDRESS OF SIGNER
TIME ☐ AM ☐ PM		
FEE	☐ PERSONAL KNOWLEDGE	
	☐ DL, PASSPORT OR OTHER ID CARD	
THUMBPRINT	☐ CREDIBLE WITNESS ID & SIGNATURE	
	ADDRESS OF NOTARY OR OTHER INFORMATION	PHONE NO./EMAIL:
		SIGNATURE OF SIGNER
		X

DOCUMENT TYPE/DATE	NOTARIZATION TYPE: ACKNOWLEDGEMENT / JURAT / OTHER	RECORD NO. 334

DATE	ID INFORMATION OR CREDIBLE WITNESS	PRINTED NAME & ADDRESS OF SIGNER
TIME ☐ AM ☐ PM		
FEE	☐ PERSONAL KNOWLEDGE	
THUMBPRINT	☐ DL, PASSPORT OR OTHER ID CARD	
	☐ CREDIBLE WITNESS ID & SIGNATURE	
	ADDRESS OF NOTARY OR OTHER INFORMATION	PHONE NO./EMAIL:
		SIGNATURE OF SIGNER
		X

DOCUMENT TYPE/DATE	NOTARIZATION TYPE: ACKNOWLEDGEMENT / JURAT / OTHER	RECORD NO. 335

DATE	ID INFORMATION OR CREDIBLE WITNESS	PRINTED NAME & ADDRESS OF SIGNER
TIME ☐ AM ☐ PM		
FEE	☐ PERSONAL KNOWLEDGE	
THUMBPRINT	☐ DL, PASSPORT OR OTHER ID CARD	
	☐ CREDIBLE WITNESS ID & SIGNATURE	
	ADDRESS OF NOTARY OR OTHER INFORMATION	PHONE NO./EMAIL:
		SIGNATURE OF SIGNER
		X

DOCUMENT TYPE/DATE	NOTARIZATION TYPE: ACKNOWLEDGEMENT / JURAT / OTHER	RECORD NO. 336

DATE	ID INFORMATION OR CREDIBLE WITNESS	PRINTED NAME & ADDRESS OF SIGNER
TIME ☐ AM ☐ PM		
FEE	☐ PERSONAL KNOWLEDGE	
THUMBPRINT	☐ DL, PASSPORT OR OTHER ID CARD	
	☐ CREDIBLE WITNESS ID & SIGNATURE	
	ADDRESS OF NOTARY OR OTHER INFORMATION	PHONE NO./EMAIL:
		SIGNATURE OF SIGNER
		X

RECORD NO. 337	DOCUMENT TYPE/DATE	NOTARIZATION TYPE: ACKNOWLEDGEMENT / JURAT / OTHER
DATE	ID INFORMATION OR CREDIBLE WITNESS	PRINTED NAME & ADDRESS OF SIGNER
TIME ☐ AM ☐ PM		
FEE	☐ PERSONAL KNOWLEDGE	
	☐ DL, PASSPORT OR OTHER ID CARD	
THUMBPRINT	☐ CREDIBLE WITNESS ID & SIGNATURE	
	ADDRESS OF NOTARY OR OTHER INFORMATION	PHONE NO./EMAIL:
		SIGNATURE OF SIGNER
		X

RECORD NO. 338	DOCUMENT TYPE/DATE	NOTARIZATION TYPE: ACKNOWLEDGEMENT / JURAT / OTHER
DATE	ID INFORMATION OR CREDIBLE WITNESS	PRINTED NAME & ADDRESS OF SIGNER
TIME ☐ AM ☐ PM		
FEE	☐ PERSONAL KNOWLEDGE	
	☐ DL, PASSPORT OR OTHER ID CARD	
THUMBPRINT	☐ CREDIBLE WITNESS ID & SIGNATURE	
	ADDRESS OF NOTARY OR OTHER INFORMATION	PHONE NO./EMAIL:
		SIGNATURE OF SIGNER
		X

RECORD NO. 339	DOCUMENT TYPE/DATE	NOTARIZATION TYPE: ACKNOWLEDGEMENT / JURAT / OTHER
DATE	ID INFORMATION OR CREDIBLE WITNESS	PRINTED NAME & ADDRESS OF SIGNER
TIME ☐ AM ☐ PM		
FEE	☐ PERSONAL KNOWLEDGE	
	☐ DL, PASSPORT OR OTHER ID CARD	
THUMBPRINT	☐ CREDIBLE WITNESS ID & SIGNATURE	
	ADDRESS OF NOTARY OR OTHER INFORMATION	PHONE NO./EMAIL:
		SIGNATURE OF SIGNER
		X

DOCUMENT TYPE/DATE	NOTARIZATION TYPE: ACKNOWLEDGEMENT / JURAT / OTHER	RECORD NO. 340

DATE	ID INFORMATION OR CREDIBLE WITNESS	PRINTED NAME & ADDRESS OF SIGNER
TIME ☐ AM ☐ PM		
FEE	☐ PERSONAL KNOWLEDGE	
THUMBPRINT	☐ DL, PASSPORT OR OTHER ID CARD ☐ CREDIBLE WITNESS ID & SIGNATURE	
	ADDRESS OF NOTARY OR OTHER INFORMATION	PHONE NO./EMAIL:
		SIGNATURE OF SIGNER X

DOCUMENT TYPE/DATE	NOTARIZATION TYPE: ACKNOWLEDGEMENT / JURAT / OTHER	RECORD NO. 341

DATE	ID INFORMATION OR CREDIBLE WITNESS	PRINTED NAME & ADDRESS OF SIGNER
TIME ☐ AM ☐ PM		
FEE	☐ PERSONAL KNOWLEDGE	
THUMBPRINT	☐ DL, PASSPORT OR OTHER ID CARD ☐ CREDIBLE WITNESS ID & SIGNATURE	
	ADDRESS OF NOTARY OR OTHER INFORMATION	PHONE NO./EMAIL:
		SIGNATURE OF SIGNER X

DOCUMENT TYPE/DATE	NOTARIZATION TYPE: ACKNOWLEDGEMENT / JURAT / OTHER	RECORD NO. 342

DATE	ID INFORMATION OR CREDIBLE WITNESS	PRINTED NAME & ADDRESS OF SIGNER
TIME ☐ AM ☐ PM		
FEE	☐ PERSONAL KNOWLEDGE	
THUMBPRINT	☐ DL, PASSPORT OR OTHER ID CARD ☐ CREDIBLE WITNESS ID & SIGNATURE	
	ADDRESS OF NOTARY OR OTHER INFORMATION	PHONE NO./EMAIL:
		SIGNATURE OF SIGNER X

RECORD NO. 343	DOCUMENT TYPE/DATE	NOTARIZATION TYPE: ACKNOWLEDGEMENT / JURAT / OTHER
DATE	ID INFORMATION OR CREDIBLE WITNESS	PRINTED NAME & ADDRESS OF SIGNER
TIME ☐ AM ☐ PM		
FEE	☐ PERSONAL KNOWLEDGE	
	☐ DL, PASSPORT OR OTHER ID CARD	
THUMBPRINT	☐ CREDIBLE WITNESS ID & SIGNATURE	
	ADDRESS OF NOTARY OR OTHER INFORMATION	PHONE NO./EMAIL:
		SIGNATURE OF SIGNER
		X

RECORD NO. 344	DOCUMENT TYPE/DATE	NOTARIZATION TYPE: ACKNOWLEDGEMENT / JURAT / OTHER
DATE	ID INFORMATION OR CREDIBLE WITNESS	PRINTED NAME & ADDRESS OF SIGNER
TIME ☐ AM ☐ PM		
FEE	☐ PERSONAL KNOWLEDGE	
	☐ DL, PASSPORT OR OTHER ID CARD	
THUMBPRINT	☐ CREDIBLE WITNESS ID & SIGNATURE	
	ADDRESS OF NOTARY OR OTHER INFORMATION	PHONE NO./EMAIL:
		SIGNATURE OF SIGNER
		X

RECORD NO. 345	DOCUMENT TYPE/DATE	NOTARIZATION TYPE: ACKNOWLEDGEMENT / JURAT / OTHER
DATE	ID INFORMATION OR CREDIBLE WITNESS	PRINTED NAME & ADDRESS OF SIGNER
TIME ☐ AM ☐ PM		
FEE	☐ PERSONAL KNOWLEDGE	
	☐ DL, PASSPORT OR OTHER ID CARD	
THUMBPRINT	☐ CREDIBLE WITNESS ID & SIGNATURE	
	ADDRESS OF NOTARY OR OTHER INFORMATION	PHONE NO./EMAIL:
		SIGNATURE OF SIGNER
		X

DOCUMENT TYPE/DATE	NOTARIZATION TYPE: ACKNOWLEDGEMENT / JURAT / OTHER	RECORD NO. 346

DATE	ID INFORMATION OR CREDIBLE WITNESS	PRINTED NAME & ADDRESS OF SIGNER
TIME ☐ AM ☐ PM		
FEE	☐ PERSONAL KNOWLEDGE	
THUMBPRINT	☐ DL, PASSPORT OR OTHER ID CARD ☐ CREDIBLE WITNESS ID & SIGNATURE	
	ADDRESS OF NOTARY OR OTHER INFORMATION	PHONE NO./EMAIL:
		SIGNATURE OF SIGNER
		X

DOCUMENT TYPE/DATE	NOTARIZATION TYPE: ACKNOWLEDGEMENT / JURAT / OTHER	RECORD NO. 347

DATE	ID INFORMATION OR CREDIBLE WITNESS	PRINTED NAME & ADDRESS OF SIGNER
TIME ☐ AM ☐ PM		
FEE	☐ PERSONAL KNOWLEDGE	
THUMBPRINT	☐ DL, PASSPORT OR OTHER ID CARD ☐ CREDIBLE WITNESS ID & SIGNATURE	
	ADDRESS OF NOTARY OR OTHER INFORMATION	PHONE NO./EMAIL:
		SIGNATURE OF SIGNER
		X

DOCUMENT TYPE/DATE	NOTARIZATION TYPE: ACKNOWLEDGEMENT / JURAT / OTHER	RECORD NO. 348

DATE	ID INFORMATION OR CREDIBLE WITNESS	PRINTED NAME & ADDRESS OF SIGNER
TIME ☐ AM ☐ PM		
FEE	☐ PERSONAL KNOWLEDGE	
THUMBPRINT	☐ DL, PASSPORT OR OTHER ID CARD ☐ CREDIBLE WITNESS ID & SIGNATURE	
	ADDRESS OF NOTARY OR OTHER INFORMATION	PHONE NO./EMAIL:
		SIGNATURE OF SIGNER
		X

RECORD NO. 349	DOCUMENT TYPE/DATE	NOTARIZATION TYPE: ACKNOWLEDGEMENT / JURAT / OTHER
DATE	ID INFORMATION OR CREDIBLE WITNESS	PRINTED NAME & ADDRESS OF SIGNER
TIME ☐ AM ☐ PM		
FEE	☐ PERSONAL KNOWLEDGE ☐ DL, PASSPORT OR OTHER ID CARD ☐ CREDIBLE WITNESS ID & SIGNATURE	
THUMBPRINT	ADDRESS OF NOTARY OR OTHER INFORMATION	PHONE NO./EMAIL:
		SIGNATURE OF SIGNER X

RECORD NO. 350	DOCUMENT TYPE/DATE	NOTARIZATION TYPE: ACKNOWLEDGEMENT / JURAT / OTHER
DATE	ID INFORMATION OR CREDIBLE WITNESS	PRINTED NAME & ADDRESS OF SIGNER
TIME ☐ AM ☐ PM		
FEE	☐ PERSONAL KNOWLEDGE ☐ DL, PASSPORT OR OTHER ID CARD ☐ CREDIBLE WITNESS ID & SIGNATURE	
THUMBPRINT	ADDRESS OF NOTARY OR OTHER INFORMATION	PHONE NO./EMAIL:
		SIGNATURE OF SIGNER X

RECORD NO. 351	DOCUMENT TYPE/DATE	NOTARIZATION TYPE: ACKNOWLEDGEMENT / JURAT / OTHER
DATE	ID INFORMATION OR CREDIBLE WITNESS	PRINTED NAME & ADDRESS OF SIGNER
TIME ☐ AM ☐ PM		
FEE	☐ PERSONAL KNOWLEDGE ☐ DL, PASSPORT OR OTHER ID CARD ☐ CREDIBLE WITNESS ID & SIGNATURE	
THUMBPRINT	ADDRESS OF NOTARY OR OTHER INFORMATION	PHONE NO./EMAIL:
		SIGNATURE OF SIGNER X

DOCUMENT TYPE/DATE	NOTARIZATION TYPE: ACKNOWLEDGEMENT / JURAT / OTHER	RECORD NO. 352

DATE	ID INFORMATION OR CREDIBLE WITNESS	PRINTED NAME & ADDRESS OF SIGNER
TIME ☐ AM ☐ PM		
FEE	☐ PERSONAL KNOWLEDGE	
	☐ DL, PASSPORT OR OTHER ID CARD	
THUMBPRINT	☐ CREDIBLE WITNESS ID & SIGNATURE	
	ADDRESS OF NOTARY OR OTHER INFORMATION	PHONE NO./EMAIL:
		SIGNATURE OF SIGNER
		X

DOCUMENT TYPE/DATE	NOTARIZATION TYPE: ACKNOWLEDGEMENT / JURAT / OTHER	RECORD NO. 353

DATE	ID INFORMATION OR CREDIBLE WITNESS	PRINTED NAME & ADDRESS OF SIGNER
TIME ☐ AM ☐ PM		
FEE	☐ PERSONAL KNOWLEDGE	
	☐ DL, PASSPORT OR OTHER ID CARD	
THUMBPRINT	☐ CREDIBLE WITNESS ID & SIGNATURE	
	ADDRESS OF NOTARY OR OTHER INFORMATION	PHONE NO./EMAIL:
		SIGNATURE OF SIGNER
		X

DOCUMENT TYPE/DATE	NOTARIZATION TYPE: ACKNOWLEDGEMENT / JURAT / OTHER	RECORD NO. 354

DATE	ID INFORMATION OR CREDIBLE WITNESS	PRINTED NAME & ADDRESS OF SIGNER
TIME ☐ AM ☐ PM		
FEE	☐ PERSONAL KNOWLEDGE	
	☐ DL, PASSPORT OR OTHER ID CARD	
THUMBPRINT	☐ CREDIBLE WITNESS ID & SIGNATURE	
	ADDRESS OF NOTARY OR OTHER INFORMATION	PHONE NO./EMAIL:
		SIGNATURE OF SIGNER
		X

RECORD NO. 355	DOCUMENT TYPE/DATE	NOTARIZATION TYPE: ACKNOWLEDGEMENT / JURAT / OTHER
DATE	ID INFORMATION OR CREDIBLE WITNESS	PRINTED NAME & ADDRESS OF SIGNER
TIME ☐ AM ☐ PM		
FEE	☐ PERSONAL KNOWLEDGE ☐ DL, PASSPORT OR OTHER ID CARD ☐ CREDIBLE WITNESS ID & SIGNATURE	
THUMBPRINT	ADDRESS OF NOTARY OR OTHER INFORMATION	PHONE NO./EMAIL:
		SIGNATURE OF SIGNER X

RECORD NO. 356	DOCUMENT TYPE/DATE	NOTARIZATION TYPE: ACKNOWLEDGEMENT / JURAT / OTHER
DATE	ID INFORMATION OR CREDIBLE WITNESS	PRINTED NAME & ADDRESS OF SIGNER
TIME ☐ AM ☐ PM		
FEE	☐ PERSONAL KNOWLEDGE ☐ DL, PASSPORT OR OTHER ID CARD ☐ CREDIBLE WITNESS ID & SIGNATURE	
THUMBPRINT	ADDRESS OF NOTARY OR OTHER INFORMATION	PHONE NO./EMAIL:
		SIGNATURE OF SIGNER X

RECORD NO. 357	DOCUMENT TYPE/DATE	NOTARIZATION TYPE: ACKNOWLEDGEMENT / JURAT / OTHER
DATE	ID INFORMATION OR CREDIBLE WITNESS	PRINTED NAME & ADDRESS OF SIGNER
TIME ☐ AM ☐ PM		
FEE	☐ PERSONAL KNOWLEDGE ☐ DL, PASSPORT OR OTHER ID CARD ☐ CREDIBLE WITNESS ID & SIGNATURE	
THUMBPRINT	ADDRESS OF NOTARY OR OTHER INFORMATION	PHONE NO./EMAIL:
		SIGNATURE OF SIGNER X

DOCUMENT TYPE/DATE	NOTARIZATION TYPE: ACKNOWLEDGEMENT / JURAT / OTHER	RECORD NO. 358

DATE	ID INFORMATION OR CREDIBLE WITNESS	PRINTED NAME & ADDRESS OF SIGNER
TIME ☐ AM ☐ PM		
FEE	☐ PERSONAL KNOWLEDGE	
	☐ DL, PASSPORT OR OTHER ID CARD	
THUMBPRINT	☐ CREDIBLE WITNESS ID & SIGNATURE	
	ADDRESS OF NOTARY OR OTHER INFORMATION	PHONE NO./EMAIL:
		SIGNATURE OF SIGNER
		X

DOCUMENT TYPE/DATE	NOTARIZATION TYPE: ACKNOWLEDGEMENT / JURAT / OTHER	RECORD NO. 359

DATE	ID INFORMATION OR CREDIBLE WITNESS	PRINTED NAME & ADDRESS OF SIGNER
TIME ☐ AM ☐ PM		
FEE	☐ PERSONAL KNOWLEDGE	
	☐ DL, PASSPORT OR OTHER ID CARD	
THUMBPRINT	☐ CREDIBLE WITNESS ID & SIGNATURE	
	ADDRESS OF NOTARY OR OTHER INFORMATION	PHONE NO./EMAIL:
		SIGNATURE OF SIGNER
		X

DOCUMENT TYPE/DATE	NOTARIZATION TYPE: ACKNOWLEDGEMENT / JURAT / OTHER	RECORD NO. 360

DATE	ID INFORMATION OR CREDIBLE WITNESS	PRINTED NAME & ADDRESS OF SIGNER
TIME ☐ AM ☐ PM		
FEE	☐ PERSONAL KNOWLEDGE	
	☐ DL, PASSPORT OR OTHER ID CARD	
THUMBPRINT	☐ CREDIBLE WITNESS ID & SIGNATURE	
	ADDRESS OF NOTARY OR OTHER INFORMATION	PHONE NO./EMAIL:
		SIGNATURE OF SIGNER
		X

RECORD NO. 361	DOCUMENT TYPE/DATE	NOTARIZATION TYPE: ACKNOWLEDGEMENT / JURAT / OTHER
DATE	ID INFORMATION OR CREDIBLE WITNESS	PRINTED NAME & ADDRESS OF SIGNER
TIME ☐ AM ☐ PM		
FEE	☐ PERSONAL KNOWLEDGE ☐ DL, PASSPORT OR OTHER ID CARD	
THUMBPRINT	☐ CREDIBLE WITNESS ID & SIGNATURE	
	ADDRESS OF NOTARY OR OTHER INFORMATION	PHONE NO./EMAIL:
		SIGNATURE OF SIGNER X

RECORD NO. 362	DOCUMENT TYPE/DATE	NOTARIZATION TYPE: ACKNOWLEDGEMENT / JURAT / OTHER
DATE	ID INFORMATION OR CREDIBLE WITNESS	PRINTED NAME & ADDRESS OF SIGNER
TIME ☐ AM ☐ PM		
FEE	☐ PERSONAL KNOWLEDGE ☐ DL, PASSPORT OR OTHER ID CARD	
THUMBPRINT	☐ CREDIBLE WITNESS ID & SIGNATURE	
	ADDRESS OF NOTARY OR OTHER INFORMATION	PHONE NO./EMAIL:
		SIGNATURE OF SIGNER X

RECORD NO. 363	DOCUMENT TYPE/DATE	NOTARIZATION TYPE: ACKNOWLEDGEMENT / JURAT / OTHER
DATE	ID INFORMATION OR CREDIBLE WITNESS	PRINTED NAME & ADDRESS OF SIGNER
TIME ☐ AM ☐ PM		
FEE	☐ PERSONAL KNOWLEDGE ☐ DL, PASSPORT OR OTHER ID CARD	
THUMBPRINT	☐ CREDIBLE WITNESS ID & SIGNATURE	
	ADDRESS OF NOTARY OR OTHER INFORMATION	PHONE NO./EMAIL:
		SIGNATURE OF SIGNER X

DOCUMENT TYPE/DATE	NOTARIZATION TYPE: ACKNOWLEDGEMENT / JURAT / OTHER	RECORD NO. 364

DATE	ID INFORMATION OR CREDIBLE WITNESS	PRINTED NAME & ADDRESS OF SIGNER
TIME ☐ AM ☐ PM		
FEE	☐ PERSONAL KNOWLEDGE	
THUMBPRINT	☐ DL, PASSPORT OR OTHER ID CARD	
	☐ CREDIBLE WITNESS ID & SIGNATURE	
	ADDRESS OF NOTARY OR OTHER INFORMATION	PHONE NO./EMAIL:
		SIGNATURE OF SIGNER
		X

DOCUMENT TYPE/DATE	NOTARIZATION TYPE: ACKNOWLEDGEMENT / JURAT / OTHER	RECORD NO. 365

DATE	ID INFORMATION OR CREDIBLE WITNESS	PRINTED NAME & ADDRESS OF SIGNER
TIME ☐ AM ☐ PM		
FEE	☐ PERSONAL KNOWLEDGE	
THUMBPRINT	☐ DL, PASSPORT OR OTHER ID CARD	
	☐ CREDIBLE WITNESS ID & SIGNATURE	
	ADDRESS OF NOTARY OR OTHER INFORMATION	PHONE NO./EMAIL:
		SIGNATURE OF SIGNER
		X

DOCUMENT TYPE/DATE	NOTARIZATION TYPE: ACKNOWLEDGEMENT / JURAT / OTHER	RECORD NO. 366

DATE	ID INFORMATION OR CREDIBLE WITNESS	PRINTED NAME & ADDRESS OF SIGNER
TIME ☐ AM ☐ PM		
FEE	☐ PERSONAL KNOWLEDGE	
THUMBPRINT	☐ DL, PASSPORT OR OTHER ID CARD	
	☐ CREDIBLE WITNESS ID & SIGNATURE	
	ADDRESS OF NOTARY OR OTHER INFORMATION	PHONE NO./EMAIL:
		SIGNATURE OF SIGNER
		X

RECORD NO. 367	DOCUMENT TYPE/DATE	NOTARIZATION TYPE: ACKNOWLEDGEMENT / JURAT / OTHER
DATE	ID INFORMATION OR CREDIBLE WITNESS	PRINTED NAME & ADDRESS OF SIGNER
TIME ☐ AM ☐ PM		
FEE	☐ PERSONAL KNOWLEDGE	
	☐ DL, PASSPORT OR OTHER ID CARD	
THUMBPRINT	☐ CREDIBLE WITNESS ID & SIGNATURE	
	ADDRESS OF NOTARY OR OTHER INFORMATION	PHONE NO./EMAIL:
		SIGNATURE OF SIGNER
		X

RECORD NO. 368	DOCUMENT TYPE/DATE	NOTARIZATION TYPE: ACKNOWLEDGEMENT / JURAT / OTHER
DATE	ID INFORMATION OR CREDIBLE WITNESS	PRINTED NAME & ADDRESS OF SIGNER
TIME ☐ AM ☐ PM		
FEE	☐ PERSONAL KNOWLEDGE	
	☐ DL, PASSPORT OR OTHER ID CARD	
THUMBPRINT	☐ CREDIBLE WITNESS ID & SIGNATURE	
	ADDRESS OF NOTARY OR OTHER INFORMATION	PHONE NO./EMAIL:
		SIGNATURE OF SIGNER
		X

RECORD NO. 369	DOCUMENT TYPE/DATE	NOTARIZATION TYPE: ACKNOWLEDGEMENT / JURAT / OTHER
DATE	ID INFORMATION OR CREDIBLE WITNESS	PRINTED NAME & ADDRESS OF SIGNER
TIME ☐ AM ☐ PM		
FEE	☐ PERSONAL KNOWLEDGE	
	☐ DL, PASSPORT OR OTHER ID CARD	
THUMBPRINT	☐ CREDIBLE WITNESS ID & SIGNATURE	
	ADDRESS OF NOTARY OR OTHER INFORMATION	PHONE NO./EMAIL:
		SIGNATURE OF SIGNER
		X

DOCUMENT TYPE/DATE	NOTARIZATION TYPE: ACKNOWLEDGEMENT / JURAT / OTHER	RECORD NO. 370

DATE	ID INFORMATION OR CREDIBLE WITNESS	PRINTED NAME & ADDRESS OF SIGNER
TIME ☐ AM ☐ PM		
FEE	☐ PERSONAL KNOWLEDGE	
	☐ DL, PASSPORT OR OTHER ID CARD	
THUMBPRINT	☐ CREDIBLE WITNESS ID & SIGNATURE	
	ADDRESS OF NOTARY OR OTHER INFORMATION	PHONE NO./EMAIL:
		SIGNATURE OF SIGNER
		X

DOCUMENT TYPE/DATE	NOTARIZATION TYPE: ACKNOWLEDGEMENT / JURAT / OTHER	RECORD NO. 371

DATE	ID INFORMATION OR CREDIBLE WITNESS	PRINTED NAME & ADDRESS OF SIGNER
TIME ☐ AM ☐ PM		
FEE	☐ PERSONAL KNOWLEDGE	
	☐ DL, PASSPORT OR OTHER ID CARD	
THUMBPRINT	☐ CREDIBLE WITNESS ID & SIGNATURE	
	ADDRESS OF NOTARY OR OTHER INFORMATION	PHONE NO./EMAIL:
		SIGNATURE OF SIGNER
		X

DOCUMENT TYPE/DATE	NOTARIZATION TYPE: ACKNOWLEDGEMENT / JURAT / OTHER	RECORD NO. 372

DATE	ID INFORMATION OR CREDIBLE WITNESS	PRINTED NAME & ADDRESS OF SIGNER
TIME ☐ AM ☐ PM		
FEE	☐ PERSONAL KNOWLEDGE	
	☐ DL, PASSPORT OR OTHER ID CARD	
THUMBPRINT	☐ CREDIBLE WITNESS ID & SIGNATURE	
	ADDRESS OF NOTARY OR OTHER INFORMATION	PHONE NO./EMAIL:
		SIGNATURE OF SIGNER
		X

RECORD NO. 373	DOCUMENT TYPE/DATE	NOTARIZATION TYPE: ACKNOWLEDGEMENT / JURAT / OTHER
DATE	ID INFORMATION OR CREDIBLE WITNESS	PRINTED NAME & ADDRESS OF SIGNER
TIME ☐ AM ☐ PM		
FEE	☐ PERSONAL KNOWLEDGE ☐ DL, PASSPORT OR OTHER ID CARD ☐ CREDIBLE WITNESS ID & SIGNATURE	
THUMBPRINT	ADDRESS OF NOTARY OR OTHER INFORMATION	PHONE NO./EMAIL:
		SIGNATURE OF SIGNER X

RECORD NO. 374	DOCUMENT TYPE/DATE	NOTARIZATION TYPE: ACKNOWLEDGEMENT / JURAT / OTHER
DATE	ID INFORMATION OR CREDIBLE WITNESS	PRINTED NAME & ADDRESS OF SIGNER
TIME ☐ AM ☐ PM		
FEE	☐ PERSONAL KNOWLEDGE ☐ DL, PASSPORT OR OTHER ID CARD ☐ CREDIBLE WITNESS ID & SIGNATURE	
THUMBPRINT	ADDRESS OF NOTARY OR OTHER INFORMATION	PHONE NO./EMAIL:
		SIGNATURE OF SIGNER X

RECORD NO. 375	DOCUMENT TYPE/DATE	NOTARIZATION TYPE: ACKNOWLEDGEMENT / JURAT / OTHER
DATE	ID INFORMATION OR CREDIBLE WITNESS	PRINTED NAME & ADDRESS OF SIGNER
TIME ☐ AM ☐ PM		
FEE	☐ PERSONAL KNOWLEDGE ☐ DL, PASSPORT OR OTHER ID CARD ☐ CREDIBLE WITNESS ID & SIGNATURE	
THUMBPRINT	ADDRESS OF NOTARY OR OTHER INFORMATION	PHONE NO./EMAIL:
		SIGNATURE OF SIGNER X

DOCUMENT TYPE/DATE	NOTARIZATION TYPE: ACKNOWLEDGEMENT / JURAT / OTHER	RECORD NO. 376

DATE	ID INFORMATION OR CREDIBLE WITNESS	PRINTED NAME & ADDRESS OF SIGNER
TIME ☐ AM ☐ PM		
FEE	☐ PERSONAL KNOWLEDGE	
	☐ DL, PASSPORT OR OTHER ID CARD	
THUMBPRINT	☐ CREDIBLE WITNESS ID & SIGNATURE	
	ADDRESS OF NOTARY OR OTHER INFORMATION	PHONE NO./EMAIL:
		SIGNATURE OF SIGNER
		X

DOCUMENT TYPE/DATE	NOTARIZATION TYPE: ACKNOWLEDGEMENT / JURAT / OTHER	RECORD NO. 377

DATE	ID INFORMATION OR CREDIBLE WITNESS	PRINTED NAME & ADDRESS OF SIGNER
TIME ☐ AM ☐ PM		
FEE	☐ PERSONAL KNOWLEDGE	
	☐ DL, PASSPORT OR OTHER ID CARD	
THUMBPRINT	☐ CREDIBLE WITNESS ID & SIGNATURE	
	ADDRESS OF NOTARY OR OTHER INFORMATION	PHONE NO./EMAIL:
		SIGNATURE OF SIGNER
		X

DOCUMENT TYPE/DATE	NOTARIZATION TYPE: ACKNOWLEDGEMENT / JURAT / OTHER	RECORD NO. 378

DATE	ID INFORMATION OR CREDIBLE WITNESS	PRINTED NAME & ADDRESS OF SIGNER
TIME ☐ AM ☐ PM		
FEE	☐ PERSONAL KNOWLEDGE	
	☐ DL, PASSPORT OR OTHER ID CARD	
THUMBPRINT	☐ CREDIBLE WITNESS ID & SIGNATURE	
	ADDRESS OF NOTARY OR OTHER INFORMATION	PHONE NO./EMAIL:
		SIGNATURE OF SIGNER
		X

RECORD NO. 379	DOCUMENT TYPE/DATE	NOTARIZATION TYPE: ACKNOWLEDGEMENT / JURAT / OTHER
DATE	ID INFORMATION OR CREDIBLE WITNESS	PRINTED NAME & ADDRESS OF SIGNER
TIME ☐ AM ☐ PM		
FEE	☐ PERSONAL KNOWLEDGE	
	☐ DL, PASSPORT OR OTHER ID CARD	
THUMBPRINT	☐ CREDIBLE WITNESS ID & SIGNATURE	
	ADDRESS OF NOTARY OR OTHER INFORMATION	PHONE NO./EMAIL:
		SIGNATURE OF SIGNER
		X

RECORD NO. 380	DOCUMENT TYPE/DATE	NOTARIZATION TYPE: ACKNOWLEDGEMENT / JURAT / OTHER
DATE	ID INFORMATION OR CREDIBLE WITNESS	PRINTED NAME & ADDRESS OF SIGNER
TIME ☐ AM ☐ PM		
FEE	☐ PERSONAL KNOWLEDGE	
	☐ DL, PASSPORT OR OTHER ID CARD	
THUMBPRINT	☐ CREDIBLE WITNESS ID & SIGNATURE	
	ADDRESS OF NOTARY OR OTHER INFORMATION	PHONE NO./EMAIL:
		SIGNATURE OF SIGNER
		X

RECORD NO. 381	DOCUMENT TYPE/DATE	NOTARIZATION TYPE: ACKNOWLEDGEMENT / JURAT / OTHER
DATE	ID INFORMATION OR CREDIBLE WITNESS	PRINTED NAME & ADDRESS OF SIGNER
TIME ☐ AM ☐ PM		
FEE	☐ PERSONAL KNOWLEDGE	
	☐ DL, PASSPORT OR OTHER ID CARD	
THUMBPRINT	☐ CREDIBLE WITNESS ID & SIGNATURE	
	ADDRESS OF NOTARY OR OTHER INFORMATION	PHONE NO./EMAIL:
		SIGNATURE OF SIGNER
		X

DOCUMENT TYPE/DATE	NOTARIZATION TYPE: ACKNOWLEDGEMENT / JURAT / OTHER	RECORD NO. 382

DATE	ID INFORMATION OR CREDIBLE WITNESS	PRINTED NAME & ADDRESS OF SIGNER
TIME ☐ AM ☐ PM		
FEE	☐ PERSONAL KNOWLEDGE	
	☐ DL, PASSPORT OR OTHER ID CARD	
THUMBPRINT	☐ CREDIBLE WITNESS ID & SIGNATURE	
	ADDRESS OF NOTARY OR OTHER INFORMATION	PHONE NO./EMAIL:
		SIGNATURE OF SIGNER
		X

DOCUMENT TYPE/DATE	NOTARIZATION TYPE: ACKNOWLEDGEMENT / JURAT / OTHER	RECORD NO. 383

DATE	ID INFORMATION OR CREDIBLE WITNESS	PRINTED NAME & ADDRESS OF SIGNER
TIME ☐ AM ☐ PM		
FEE	☐ PERSONAL KNOWLEDGE	
	☐ DL, PASSPORT OR OTHER ID CARD	
THUMBPRINT	☐ CREDIBLE WITNESS ID & SIGNATURE	
	ADDRESS OF NOTARY OR OTHER INFORMATION	PHONE NO./EMAIL:
		SIGNATURE OF SIGNER
		X

DOCUMENT TYPE/DATE	NOTARIZATION TYPE: ACKNOWLEDGEMENT / JURAT / OTHER	RECORD NO. 384

DATE	ID INFORMATION OR CREDIBLE WITNESS	PRINTED NAME & ADDRESS OF SIGNER
TIME ☐ AM ☐ PM		
FEE	☐ PERSONAL KNOWLEDGE	
	☐ DL, PASSPORT OR OTHER ID CARD	
THUMBPRINT	☐ CREDIBLE WITNESS ID & SIGNATURE	
	ADDRESS OF NOTARY OR OTHER INFORMATION	PHONE NO./EMAIL:
		SIGNATURE OF SIGNER
		X

RECORD NO. 385	DOCUMENT TYPE/DATE	NOTARIZATION TYPE: ACKNOWLEDGEMENT / JURAT / OTHER
DATE	ID INFORMATION OR CREDIBLE WITNESS	PRINTED NAME & ADDRESS OF SIGNER
TIME ☐ AM ☐ PM		
FEE	☐ PERSONAL KNOWLEDGE ☐ DL, PASSPORT OR OTHER ID CARD ☐ CREDIBLE WITNESS ID & SIGNATURE	
THUMBPRINT	ADDRESS OF NOTARY OR OTHER INFORMATION	PHONE NO./EMAIL:
		SIGNATURE OF SIGNER X

RECORD NO. 386	DOCUMENT TYPE/DATE	NOTARIZATION TYPE: ACKNOWLEDGEMENT / JURAT / OTHER
DATE	ID INFORMATION OR CREDIBLE WITNESS	PRINTED NAME & ADDRESS OF SIGNER
TIME ☐ AM ☐ PM		
FEE	☐ PERSONAL KNOWLEDGE ☐ DL, PASSPORT OR OTHER ID CARD ☐ CREDIBLE WITNESS ID & SIGNATURE	
THUMBPRINT	ADDRESS OF NOTARY OR OTHER INFORMATION	PHONE NO./EMAIL:
		SIGNATURE OF SIGNER X

RECORD NO. 387	DOCUMENT TYPE/DATE	NOTARIZATION TYPE: ACKNOWLEDGEMENT / JURAT / OTHER
DATE	ID INFORMATION OR CREDIBLE WITNESS	PRINTED NAME & ADDRESS OF SIGNER
TIME ☐ AM ☐ PM		
FEE	☐ PERSONAL KNOWLEDGE ☐ DL, PASSPORT OR OTHER ID CARD ☐ CREDIBLE WITNESS ID & SIGNATURE	
THUMBPRINT	ADDRESS OF NOTARY OR OTHER INFORMATION	PHONE NO./EMAIL:
		SIGNATURE OF SIGNER X

DOCUMENT TYPE/DATE	NOTARIZATION TYPE: ACKNOWLEDGEMENT / JURAT / OTHER	RECORD NO. 388

DATE	ID INFORMATION OR CREDIBLE WITNESS	PRINTED NAME & ADDRESS OF SIGNER
TIME ☐ AM ☐ PM		
FEE	☐ PERSONAL KNOWLEDGE	
	☐ DL, PASSPORT OR OTHER ID CARD	
THUMBPRINT	☐ CREDIBLE WITNESS ID & SIGNATURE	
	ADDRESS OF NOTARY OR OTHER INFORMATION	PHONE NO./EMAIL:
		SIGNATURE OF SIGNER
		X

DOCUMENT TYPE/DATE	NOTARIZATION TYPE: ACKNOWLEDGEMENT / JURAT / OTHER	RECORD NO. 389

DATE	ID INFORMATION OR CREDIBLE WITNESS	PRINTED NAME & ADDRESS OF SIGNER
TIME ☐ AM ☐ PM		
FEE	☐ PERSONAL KNOWLEDGE	
	☐ DL, PASSPORT OR OTHER ID CARD	
THUMBPRINT	☐ CREDIBLE WITNESS ID & SIGNATURE	
	ADDRESS OF NOTARY OR OTHER INFORMATION	PHONE NO./EMAIL:
		SIGNATURE OF SIGNER
		X

DOCUMENT TYPE/DATE	NOTARIZATION TYPE: ACKNOWLEDGEMENT / JURAT / OTHER	RECORD NO. 390

DATE	ID INFORMATION OR CREDIBLE WITNESS	PRINTED NAME & ADDRESS OF SIGNER
TIME ☐ AM ☐ PM		
FEE	☐ PERSONAL KNOWLEDGE	
	☐ DL, PASSPORT OR OTHER ID CARD	
THUMBPRINT	☐ CREDIBLE WITNESS ID & SIGNATURE	
	ADDRESS OF NOTARY OR OTHER INFORMATION	PHONE NO./EMAIL:
		SIGNATURE OF SIGNER
		X

NOTES

CPSIA information can be obtained
at www.ICGtesting.com
Printed in the USA
BVHW091305171121
621767BV00003B/499